Thomas Robinson Warren

Shooting, Boating and Fishing

For Young Sportsmen

Thomas Robinson Warren

Shooting, Boating and Fishing
For Young Sportsmen

ISBN/EAN: 9783337412920

Printed in Europe, USA, Canada, Australia, Japan

Cover: Foto ©Lupo / pixelio.de

More available books at **www.hansebooks.com**

SHOOTING,

BOATING AND FISHING,

FOR

YOUNG SPORTSMEN.

BY

T. ROBINSON WARREN.

––––––––––

NEW YORK:

CHARLES SCRIBNER & CO

1871.

Press of ROGERS & SHERWOOD,
94 & 96 Nassau St., N. Y.

DEDICATION.

THIS BOOK I DEDICATE TO MY THREE BOYS,
JOHN, SCHUYLER, AND KEARNY,
WITH THE HOPE IT WILL LEAD THEM TO THE
CULTIVATION OF MANLY SPORTS.

THEIR FATHER.

TO MY BOYS.

Boys, so you want to be sportsmen, do you? Well, its a laudable ambition. Now do you know that there are two words in the English language which have no synonym in any other, both pleasant to the ear, not only of boyhood, but manhood, too; the one is the dear old word *home*, and the other that vigorous monosyllable *sport*. While the French have their *jeu*, the Spaniards their *juego*, and the Germans their *spiel*, all signifying a game or play, neither word possesses the comprehensiveness of the Saxon word which applies equally to the frolics of the play-ground and the sterner excitement of the chase. In proof of this, let me remark that the Parisians, some time since, determining upon the establishment of a newspaper in the interests of the sporting community, cast about them for a suitable title; it must be short, sharp, expressive. Was there no fit word or combination of words in that language so fertile, so luxuriant in idiom? It seems not, for the proprietors fell back in despair upon the English, and dubbed their new journal "Le Sport."

This word so noble, yet so simple, has been prostituted to the basest uses, for as the hypocrite adopts religion as a cloak for his misdeeds, so the gambler, the prize-fighter and the jockey strive to give themselves an air of respectability by the assumption of the title of "sporting men," but the pinchbeck is too vulgar not to be easy distinguishable from the genuine. Bear in mind, Boys, that there is nothing in the character of the *real* sportsman that is inconsistent with that of the Christian gentleman; and, also, that sportsmanship does not consist merely in shouldering a gun, following a dog across a stubble field, or casting a fly into a shady pool. Do not imagine that one is born a sportsman and has only to *buy* the implements of the trade to become an expert, for experience will teach you that few callings require so arduous an apprenticeship, combining the severe physical training of the athlete with the intellectual assiduity of the student, and that he who attains such perfection earns a proud position in the ranks of manhood. Sportsmanship brooks no tampering with nature's laws, no association with vice. A clear eye and a steady hand can not coëxist with the use of artificial stimulants, nor is self-reliance or self-control the attribute of the sybarite, the gourmand, or the sensualist. The glance along the gun-barrel must be undimmed and unwavering; the grasp upon the tiller must be firm and unfaltering, and the muscle that wields the paddle or bends the oar must be of whip-cord and of steel.

As sportsmanship demands the highest physical development, so does it call for a cultivated intellect and a practical acquaintanceship with nature's laws, success in the chase requiring familiarity with the genus and variety of the game which is hunted, with its habits and its instincts, with its food and the circumstances of climate and of soil producing it.

Mechanical skill, too, to a certain extent, is essential to the sportsman, giving him a thorough knowledge of, and ability to repair, the implements of the chase; in fact he should be an amateur gunsmith, and sufficiently a sailor to fish a spar, splice a rope, or mend a sail.

Now, Boys, don't turn away in disgust, saying you don't aspire to perfection, but only want to shoot moderately well, to be able to work a dog, or cast a fly like a gentleman; and that as to sailing your own yacht, your boat-keeper is paid for doing that. Depend upon it, Boys, that whatever is worth doing at all is worth doing well, and that the pleasure that excellence affords more than compensates for the labor of its attainment. A true sportsman is independent of the gunner, who is the necessary and expensive attendant of the amateur, to whose whim and caprice he is always subject, or of the sailing master, who is usually his tyrant; the gunner generally reserving the best shooting for himself, while the sailing master is invariably ready with some quibble of impending gale or an unfavorable tide as an excuse for not getting under way when it suits his convenience to remain ashore.

Bear in mind that I do not pretend to the title of Sportsman myself, or even to that of "good shot;" but, acknowledging to an enthusiastic love of sport, (which in most of its phases I have enjoyed in the four quarters of the globe) I think myself justified in offering you the following suggestions, the result, generally speaking, of my own personal experience, hoping it may excite a sufficient interest to induce you to study such authorities as Audubon, Hawker, Herbert, Scott, Wilson, Youatt, Rosevelt and others, who, as naturalists and sportsmen, stand preëminent.

YOUR FATHER.

New Brunswick, N. J., July 4, 1871.

CONTENTS.

LIST OF ILLUSTRATIONS.

GUNPOWDER.

As GUNPOWDER plays a most important rôle in sporting matters, suppose that we pause for a moment and look into its nature and mode of manufacture. On reflection, you will agree with me in thinking it not a little strange that although Gunpowder was possibly known in very remote ages to the Chinese, and was certainly used in Europe as early as the 13th century, there should have been so little improvement made in its quality since the first invention until a very recent period; and this seems especially strange when we take into consideration that all explosive arms, so to speak, used for offense and defense, which for years have exercised the inventive genius of mankind, have naturally been dependent on its excellence for success. It is unnecessary to state that Gunpowder is the result of a combination of sulphur, saltpeter and charcoal, and I will hence endeavor to give a general outline of its manufacture in a very few words : Saltpeter, which constitutes 75 per cent. of Gunpowder, is composed of six equal parts of oxygen, one of nitrogen, and one of potasium.   This salt appears in minute crystals on the damp ground in India (and indeed in other countries in limited quantities), is collected and purified by boiling, and then shipped to Europe and to this country, and there refined by various elaborate processes until fitted for use.

The next ingredient is sulphur, which is obtained from volcanic districts, and from iron and copper pyrites.   It is purified by melting and then ground into powder and filtered through very fine seives.   It ignites at a very low temperature, and by its non-absorbent qualities it renders powder more durable.   The quantity used is from 9 @ 12½ per cent.   Charcoal is the last ingredient, and the woods used in its preparation are selected with very great care.   After carbonization it is thoroughly ground and sifted and is then ready for use.

The three ingredients are now weighed out in the following proportions, viz. :

Saltpeter,	-	-	-	-	-	75 parts.
Sulphur,	-	-	-	-	-	10 parts.
Charcoal,	-	-	-	-	-	15 parts.

and, after being mixed, about 50 ℔ weight is put into a close box, in which a drum armed with

long teeth rapidly revolves, and the mixture being perfect it is run into a bag and is termed,
technically, the *Green Charge*. It is then taken
into the incorporating mill and is put into a huge
iron dish, around which revolve runners weighing several tons; this immense pressure and action, aided by occasional applications of water,
form the mixture into a compact mass of a grayish hue. The operation lasts many hours, at the
expiration of which the mass becomes in reality
Gunpowder, but is called *Mill-cake*, and is placed
in receptacles in readiness for the next process,
which consists in taking it to the press-house and
putting it under hydraulic pressure, where the
cake, by very complicated machinery and a pressure of several hundred tons, is compressed within three-fifths of its original bulk. It is then by
another machine again broken into lumps about
as large as a hickory nut. It now goes to the
corning-house or granulating mill, where it is
converted into grains by means of immensely
heavy toothed rollers rapidly revolving; but it has
still to be glazed in order to overcome its porous-
ness, and is placed in large cylinders, which ro-
tate with great rapidity, and consequently the
grains are driven against each other with excessive force, this action generating a certain heat,

and this heat affects the color which, from a grayish tint, is converted into a glossy black, the glaze being caused by attrition, and thus the pores are closed, the surface hardened and the powder so cleaned "as not to soil the whitest glove." The foregoing is, of course, but the faintest and most imperfect description of the mode of manufacture, but it may excite your interest (and I hope it will) sufficiently to induce you to look into the matter thoroughly; only let me advise you to get your information from *books*, and not to go within five miles of a powder mill if you can possibly avoid it, for they have a way of blowing up at the most inconvenient and unexpected times, and often without the slightest possible pretext or excuse. Gunpowder is to be found in every variety, from abominably bad to the very finest quality, but a sportsman can readily distinguish the bad from the good. In the first place the color and the appearance of the powder will indicate the quality to a certain extent, then again by rubbing it briskly in the palm of the hand, if it leaves a dirty stain of course its quality is inferior; and, again, flashing it in a glass plate will show whether or not the combination is perfect, or if it is likely to foul a gun And its strength can be easily determined by actual trial with a gun ; for instance, by making a target of twenty or thirty sheets of blotting paper and firing the same charge of shot and the same charge of different brands of powder you will be able to judge of the penetration to a nicety. Sporting powders are generally made from No. 1 to No. 6, the grain increasing in size with the *number*. This, I believe, is always the mode practiced by Englishmen; but, if I mistake not, some of our American manufacturers reverse the method. I myself invariably use English powder made by Curtis & Harvey, believing, from long observation, that it is more uniform in its great strength and excessive cleanliness than any American powder.

There is no doubt that the Hazard and Dupont Mills produce a powder possessing both of these qualities in the highest degree, but they do not *always* do so, and hence I know many sportsmen who uniformly pay $1.75 per ℔. for Curtis & Harvey, when they could buy either Hazard's or Dupont's for 80 @ 90c.—the one they *know* is always up to the mark, the other may or may not be.

Of one thing I feel assured, however, and that is that there can be no good reason why English powder should be superior to the American, and as the inferiority of the latter is not the general rule, it must result from carelessness.

THE GUN.

Mrs. Partington, a very eccentric and much misrepresented old lady, has been wont to say that "a gun was dangerous without lock, stock, or barrel," and, barring a little extravagance in diction, she was about half right, for guns of unheard of age, knocked and bruised out of all semblance to fire arms, and that have lain for years in damp wet cellars, have been known to explode contrary to every known law regulating combustion.—In fact, Boys! always look upon your gun as your best friend and your worst enemy, ready to serve you if you watch it closely, but let your vigilance once cease and an instant's carelessness may cost you your life or a limb. You may think it strange Boys, but I here venture to assert that out of ten men who shoot, there shall be at least three who can not name *all* the parts of a gun that are exposed to view, let alone those that are not; it is indeed astonishing that so many men who shoot a good deal, and

are fair shots, should manifest so little interest in
the construction of their guns, relying entirely
upon their gunsmith to clean and keep them in
condition and repair ; but let me strongly advise
you to avoid any such indifference, and to make
yourselves thoroughly acquainted with every part
of your piece, and to this end I have made a
drawing of the lock and of its parts separately
and accompany it with instructions for taking it
to pieces and putting it together.

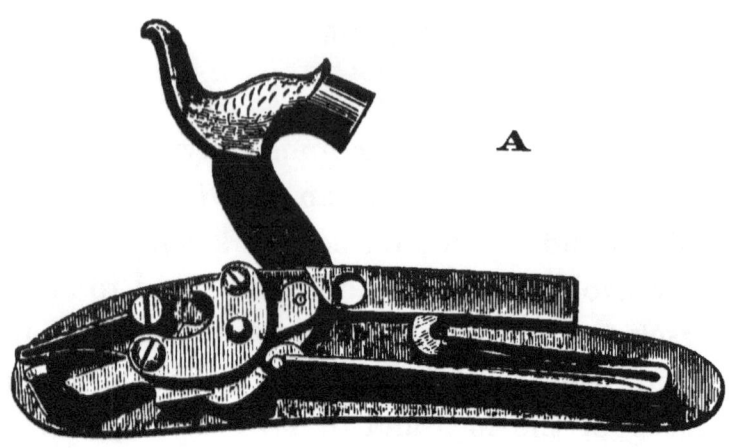

A

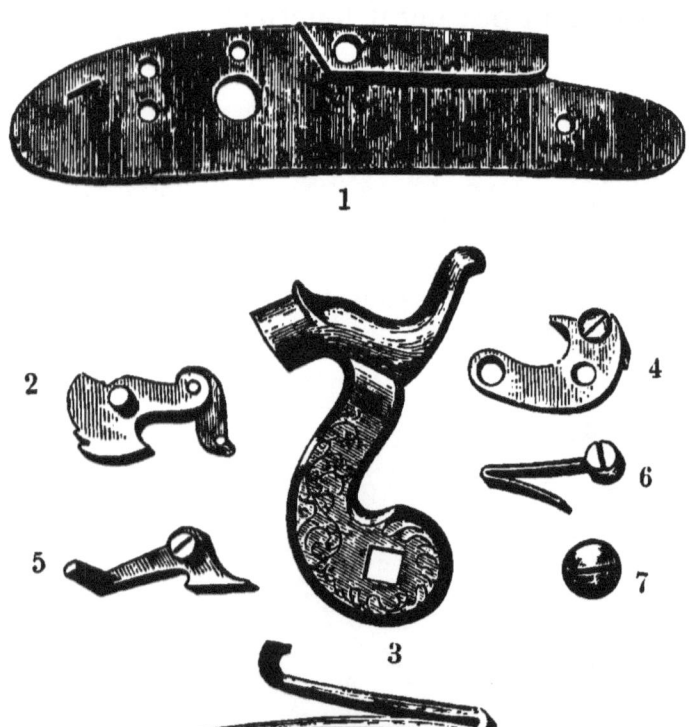

1

2

5

3

4

6

7

8

Lock Plate, No. 1.—Outside of lock.

Tumbler, No. 2.—Moveable center piece.

Hammer, No. 3.—Piece which strikes the caps.

Bridle, No. 4.—Piece which caps the tumbler and holds lock together.

Scear, No. 5.—Piece which catches tumbler on the hammer being moved to half cock.

Scear Spring, No. 6.—Small spring holding scear in the notches of the tumbler at full or half cock.

Spring Cramp.—An instrument for taking off and repairing mainspring of gun lock.

Tumbler Screw.—Outside screw securing hammer to tumbler.

Bolt.—Small piece of steel securing the barrels to the stock.

Breech.—The piece at the end of the barrels which contains the chamber.

Butt.—The end of the stock placed against the shoulder.

False Breech.—The iron on the gun stock into which the breech fits.

Chamber.—Place in the breech where the powder explodes.

Rib.—Raised piece of metal on upper side of and between barrels.

Guard.—The metal scroll which guards the triggers.

Nipple.—The tubes for caps.

Worm.—Screw at end of ramrod.

Having given you the technical names of the various parts of a gun, I will now proceed to tell you in detail how

"TO TAKE THE LOCK *to pieces.*

First.—Cramp and remove *mainspring, No.* 8, by raising the *hammer, No.* 3, to full cock, applying spring cramp and screwing it up until the hammer is powerless.

Secondly.—Press the *scear, No.* 5, and letting down the hammer, the *mainspring, No.* 8, may be taken off.

Thirdly.—Ease up the screw of the scear spring and throw it out of its mortice, after which remove screw and take out scear spring.

Fourthly.—Remove screw which fastens the Scear through the *bridle No.* 4, then remove screw holding the bridle.

Fifthly.—Remove screw holding the hammer.

Sixthly.—Then drive out the *tumbler, No.* 2.

TO ASSEMBLE OR PUT LOCK TOGETHER AGAIN.

First.—Put the *tumbler, No.* 2, into the *plate, No.* 1.

Second.—Then put on the *bridle, No.* 4, and fasten it.

Third.—Put in *scear No.* 5, with screw.

Fourth.—Then place *scear spring* into its place, and these being adjusted,

Fifth.—Put *hammer*, *No.* 3, in its place and screw
down.

Sixth.—The *mainspring*, *No.* 8, may then be re-
placed. Then hook it in the *swivel* and slip
pivot in position, and the Lock is adjusted.

Assuming that you have familiarized yourselves somewhat with the foregoing explanation,
let me advise you to look up some old fowling-
piece, and after providing yourselves with a vial
of kerosene oil (which will loosen any screw,
however obstinately rusted in,) and screw-driver,
to remove the lock, and, following the instructions, take it apart piece by piece; this will give
you a practical insight into its construction, and
after repeating the operation a few times you
will never thereafter experience any difficulty.
Having mastered this, the next thing to take
into consideration is the proper manner of

LOADING.

And, before making any suggestions in this regard, let me here say to you that more accidents
happen, while performing this operation than at
any other time or from any other cause; hence I
would endeavor to impress upon you the necessity of systematically observing a few simple
rules.

First, and above all things and always, keep

the muzzle turned away from your person; of course, while loading, your piece will be grasped in the left hand, and ought to make an angle of 45 degrees with the ground on which it rests.

Secondly; under whatever circumstances you may be placed, never allow yourself to be unduly hurried or flurried while loading, or the most unfortunate results may follow; no matter if a hundred ducks or geese be coming straight at you; no matter if both your dogs be standing stiff as pokers on separate bevies; no matter if a grizzly bear be making for you, for so sure as you do, you will make some fatal blunder and render your gun useless; you will either shove in a wad before the powder, pour in the shot first, or mayhap put both loads into one barrel, under either of which contingencies the ducks and geese would pass unharmed, the covies disappear, the grizzly dine off of you, or the gun burst and blow your brains out.

Keep cool then by all means and if you have not used your gun lately, explode a cap on the nipples to see that they are clear, then put a charge of powder into either barrel, ramming down the wads briskly upon the powder, then put a charge of shot into your right hand barrel, ramming down the wad upon *it* and LEAVING THE

2

ROD IN THE BARREL, and after putting a charge into the second barrel, ram *it* down. The object of leaving the rod in the one barrel while you are charging the other being to render it impossible to put in a DOUBLE charge, which beginners are apt to do, and which is sometimes attended with dangerous and always with disagreeable consequences.

After both barrels are loaded, replace the rod and cap the tubes, allowing the hammers to press lightly upon the eaps to see if they are well down on the nipples, and then draw them back at half cock, ALWAYS LEAVING them in that position, except at the instant before drawing up to your shoulder to fire, when, of course, they should be placed at full cock.

Now, both barrels being loaded, let us suppose that a bird gets up and is fired at, of course the exploded barrel must be reloaded; this is the time when the greatest care should be exercised, for now one hammer is at full cock and one on the nipple. In the excitement of the moment never lose sight of this fact, but always put the hammer of the unexploded barrel at half cock, otherwise, even with the greatest precaution, the mere jar of loading might explode the gun.

Having made the foregoing simple suggestions

about loading your piece, let me impress upon you the necessity of *always*

"KEEPING YOUR GUN IN GOOD CONDITION."

This you will accomplish only by always cleaning it thoroughly after use. Be you ever so wearied after a day's sport, never set your gun on one side without first swabbing it out and wiping it on the outside with a woolen rag until all moisture is removed. Mind you, I do not advise you to take off the locks unless you are going to put it away for some time, or unless you have been out in the rain or otherwise got it wet, or where the fine sand may have been driving in your vicinity, in which last event it is always desirable to remove the locks, and even to take them to pieces, as it is really wonderful how the fine grains of sand will work their way into the closest fitting locks, and of course nothing will do them so much injury if permitted to remain. The process of cleaning a gun is so very simple as to make neglect in doing it inexcusable. Of course every gunner has his cleaning rod and fixtures, his woolen rags and bottle of lubricating oil. First, then, remove the barrels from the stock, then with the wrench take off the nipples, then placing the breech of the gun in a basin of water (hot is best) pour the water through a funnel into the barrels, then swab out; working the swab up and down until the water is entirely ejected through the nipples; repeat this until the water runs through perfectly clean and clear, then attach a piece of dry woolen cloth to the screw at the end of the cleaning rod and swab with it until the barrels are perfectly dry. The nipples should then be cleaned and thoroughly dried (the screws moistened with oil) and screwed tightly into their places. The barrels should then be oiled and wiped perfectly dry and put in their place, a wad being inserted in each barrel about $\frac{1}{4}$ of an inch below the muzzle; and, previously to letting the hammers down on the nipples, a piece of buck skin should be placed over them, thus excluding the air entirely from the barrel. The gun is now supposed to be clean, but should any specks of rust be observed a drop or two of kerosene oil will remove them at once. When a gun is laid on one side for the day it should be placed in its woolen cover, but if lain away for a longer time it should be put in its leather case, as it will then be out of harm's way. * * * *

Now, then, about

"THE CHOICE OF A GUN,"

and the question immediately suggests itself, shall it be Muzzle or Breech-loading? This is dangerous ground to tread upon, for if you were to ask the advice of twenty different sportsmen, probably ten would tell you to buy a Breech-loader and ten would advise your sticking to the Muzzle-loader. Both systems have their adherents, but notwithstanding the diversity of opinion and a certain prejudice against the Breech-loader, I say, " *Boys, buy yourselves Breech-loaders.* Firstly and *principally* because they are less dangerous than the Muzzle-loading gun; and, secondly, because they give the beginner so many more chances of making a good Bag, and also for practice; for the trouble of loading a Muzzle-loader being considerable he will hesitate about shooting off his load, whereas, with a Breech-loader, knowing it to be the work of a second only, he fires away whenever there is the slightest show. In upland shooting, where speed in loading is of less consequence, the diminution in risk, both in the act of loading as well as in climbing fences, etc. (for with the Breech-loader, under such circumstances, the load is withdrawn), is a great desideratum.

The opponents of the Breech-loader assert that

there is danger of the charge blowing out at the Breech—bosh! Of course the charge will explode, in the direction of the least resistance—the breech is the stoutest part of the gun, whereas nothing intervenes between the powder in the cartridge and the *muzzle* of the gun but a charge of shot and two wads, hence in the nature of things the explosive forces will find vent in that direction.

They assert also that the loading of the shells is a dangerous and disagreeable operation. Bosh again!—there is no accident so far as I know on record, and nothing so relieves the tedium of a wet day when shooting is impracticable, or the ennui consequent upon a few spare hours at a country tavern, as the interest attendant upon the operation. The assertion that carrying loaded cartridges in a belt is hazardous, is equally preposterous, for the belt may fall a hundred times without danger to the owner, and ten to one that out of a dozen loaded cartridges that may be dropped from a two story window, not one will explode. If a person be fastidious or lazy, he may buy his cartridges already loaded at a price altogether insignificant.

It is further asserted that a Breech-loader will not shoot so sharp as a Muzzle-loader, the quality of the two guns being the same; granted, but for upland shooting, for bay or English snipe, the one is absolutely as effective as the other; for ducks, geese, and swan, or for deer, I must confess I would give the preference to the Muzzle-loader, although the Breech-loader at the ordinary range will kill as often. In fact, the facility with which the Breech-loader can be charged, the frequency with which it can be discharged, the ease with which it can be cleaned, and the facility with which one charge can be substituted for another, to suit the game that may be approaching, are arguments which must weigh heavily with a gunner: for instance, you are shooting ducks, broadbill principally, and are loaded up with No. 4 shot, suddenly, however, you spy a bunch of geese heading in over the beach and coming directly for your stand—a single motion of your body would be fatal to your shot, so, of course, if you have a Muzzle-loader, you can only take the chance of winging one with the No. 4 shot, but if you have a Breech-loader, without a perceptible motion, so far as the game is concerned, you lay your hand upon a couple of cartridges marked B B, and substituting them for the "No. 4's," you are ready to let drive before the birds have reached you.

Again, a gun is never so dangerous as when climbing fences, or when getting in and out of boats; this danger is entirely to be avoided, if you have a Breech-loader, for the process of loading and unloading being instantaneous, none but an idiot would omit withdrawing the charge under such circumstances.

The assertion that a Breech-loader *can not* be made to shoot so sharp as a Muzzle-loader is, I think, correct, for this reason, as it seems to me, *i. e.*, in charging the Muzzle-loader, a chemically prepared wad is forced down upon the powder, hermetically sealing it in the barrel, thus when the spark from the cap reaches the powder and ignites it, its *entire explosive* force is directed against the shot, there being no room for its escape; but with the Breech-loader, on the contrary, the cartridge must fit with sufficient looseness in the barrel to be inserted easily; the result is, that simultaneously with the explosion, a certain portion of gas escapes *along with instead of acting directly upon* the charge of shot. Now then, the choice of the gun rests with yourselves, but whether it be muzzle or breech-loading, choose one with as little ornamentation or gimcrackery about it as possible. All these exquisite engravings of impossible looking woodcocks, dyspeptic looking setters and cockney sportsmen traced upon the locks and barrels are either emblematic of by-gone ages, or are a temptation and a snare for young sportsmen and a receptacle for rust and dirt, for the plainer the gun the easier to keep clean; an oiled walnut stock being far preferable to one of polished mahogany.

Beyond the very manifest necessity of a long stocked gun for a long armed man, and vice-versa, there is no rule to be laid down as to the choice of a gun, so far as its peculiar form goes, —the piece that seems to balance in your hands, as you draw it quickly up on an object, is the gun that will suit you the best, but you should be thoroughly satisfied in this regard before you buy; a few hours in the field, a shot at swallows, or half a dozen pigeons from a trap, will settle the matter conclusively—indeed no respectable gunseller will object to such trial. Guns are stocked in different ways, some straight, some more or less crooked. This, however, is a mere matter of fancy; a straight breech seems to me, however, to be the more natural form.

The size of your gun, of course, depends upon the game to be pursued, but it is a safe rule to lay down that a No. 12 guage is suitable for all

2*

upland bird shooting and for bay snipe, but for
ducks and geese or swan, a No. 8 guage is about
the thing—these are good standard sizes for the
purposes named. There are sportsmen who use
but one gun, a No. 10 guage, heavy in the breech,
which, if a superior sharp-shooting gun, will
answer the purpose to a certain extent, but it
carries with it the objection, that in upland
shooting its weight becomes distressing on a
long day's tramp, and when subjected to the
heavy charges necessarily used in wild-fowl
shooting, the recoil must not only jar one pain-
fully, but also affect the accuracy of the aim.
As regards length of barrel, it is generally con-
ceded that it should be anywhere between twenty-
eight and thirty-two inches, the old idea of great
length giving increased range being thoroughly
exploded. A light No. 12 gun will weigh say
7½ lbs, having a 28 inch barrel, whereas a duck
gun, No: 8 guage, weighing 14 lbs., with a barrel
of same length, would be entirely out of propor-
tion, as two-thirds of the weight would be in the
breech and she would not balance; but give her
four inches more barrel and the balance would
be perfect.

The great desideratum with gunmakers is, of
course, to *increase* the range and to decrease the

recoil, but the former is only effected by increase of charge of powder, which, of course, augments the recoil; to counteract this, gunsmiths are now making their guns much heavier in the breech than formerly. I would strongly advise you to bear this in mind in purchasing, and not to let a pound or two extra weight be an objection, provided it be expended in the proper direction.

Thus you will see that there is no one thing in which a young sportsman should evince more circumspection and deliberation than in the choice of his gun, and, as before remarked, he should never decide upon one before thoroughly testing its shooting qualities and its peculiar adaptability to his eye and shoulder. Perhaps there is no one branch of mechanical art in which swindling is so openly and shamelessly carried on as in the manufacture and sale of fowling pieces; Belgian, German, and French makers, emulous of the fame of Westly-Richards, Manton, and other celebrities, have flooded the continent and this country with counterfeit guns, bearing their trade mark, and so dexterous is the imitation, and the guns seemingly so beautifully constructed, that only the eye of an expert can detect it. Unfortunately too, gunsellers in this country lend themselves to this deceit, and

palm off these guns as genuine. Almost all the
guns used in this country are manufactured
abroad; still we have several good makers here,
and it is doubtful whether a first-rate London
maker can turn out a better gun than can Patrick
Mullen or his brother John, of New York, or
Evans, of Philadelphia. The favorite English
makers with us, are Westly-Richards, Purdey,
Manton, Wm. Greener, Moore & Harris, Lancas-
ter, Scott, Pope, beside many others who are not
so well known. Guns turned out by these men,
of course vary greatly in price, ranging all the
way from $100 @ $500, but it is safe to say that
a gun turned out by Westly-Richards, Manton,
or Purdey, for $150, is quite as good for general
use as one costing $500, which is a mere fancy
price.

One thing you should bear in mind that a
cheap gun *is never cheap.* Guns may be bought
for $20, and in the hands of a professional may
shoot side by side with your Purdey and beat it,
but if your Purdey were in the hands of the professional, and YOU were shooting the cheap gun,
the "Purdey" would win. Cheap guns are
liable, at any moment, to burst and blow your
brains out, and the locks never can be depended
upon and are just as likely to go off at *half* as at

full *cock*. You can form some idea of what a good gun costs to the maker, when I tell you that a pair of Brazier locks alone cost over $40.*

English barrels are all tested by government and stamped before they are permitted to be sold, so that bursting under ordinary circumstances is not likely with them; but unfortunately German, Belgian and French makers counterfeit the English government proof stamp on their guns.

If you are in New York and want a gun go to Cooper, Harris & Hodgkins, in Broadway, near Cortlandt St., and ask Mr. Hodgkins' advice, and I will guarantee you will be fairly and pleasantly dealt with.

Now, Boys, you've got your gun, we'll suppose, having been told where to buy it, and how to load it and take care of it, so we will pass on to your gunning costume and to your equipment. As regards the latter, you ought to have a separate outfit as you have a separate gun, for upland and bay shooting, respectively. First and foremost you want a good English leather guncase, for no sportsman who can afford it will use anything else, for a woolen case is no protection

* Having once closely examined and manipulated a pair of fine locks, you never need be at a loss to discriminate, for they work as softly and as smoothly as a musical box.

to a gun in traveling about; a fall from car or stage-coach with such a cover would of course, in nine cases out of ten, ruin it; then, again, in a woolen case, the gun not being taken apart is awkward to carry from its length.

There has recently been a case invented, made of the best materials, in which the barrels rest upon the stock instead of being placed alongside of it, thus reducing the width of the case and making it compact as possible. This case can be bought at $25 and will last forever. The next purchase to be made is your powder-flask for upland shooting, which ought to hold $\frac{1}{2}$ lb., and shot pouch of $2\frac{1}{2}$ lbs. capacity. For bay shooting your flask should have a capacity of 1 lb., and your pouch of 5 lbs.; but above all don't buy a *shot-belt*, they are an abomination, and their inventor should *harri-kari* himself or be burned at the stake, for in loading from them you have not only to hold your gun in an absurdly awkward position, but you must have both muzzles directed point blank at your bread-basket, so in the event of an explosion you will be torn to pieces in the most improved style. The best pouches and flasks are made by Dixon & Son, covered with shark or pig skin, and tipped with German silver or brass. The dearest articles of this kind are

cheapest in the end, for a good one will last a
life time, and a cheap one may not last a week.
You also want a good ebony cleaning-rod with
the accompaniments of screw, swab, etc., a nipple
wrench and a couple of extra nipples for each
gun; all these you can stow away in the end of
your gun case. The best rig for upland shooting
is corduroy, it is both warm and cool and the
toughest material you can buy, but for summer
shooting heavy linen drilling is the best, it is cool
and very tough; the coat should be made as a
sack, very loose, with breast pockets for powder
and shot, side pocket (not too deep) for caps,
and capacious pockets either side of the skirt, as
also a large game pocket to button on the inside
of the skirt taking its entire width; a light felt
hat and a pair of stout walking boots with soft
woolen socks for the autumn, or a pair of very
old and hole-y boots for the summer shooting.

For duck shooting more elaborate preparations
are necessary, although the same corduroy suit
may be used, warmth being insured by very
heavy woolen undergarments. As the weather
at the season for such shooting is not only cold,
but wet and boisterous, it is most advisable to
have an outer suit of water-proof, and the very
best material is that used by seamen, made of

oiled cloth (not oil-cloth), the color of the clothes after a few times worn being just about the hue of the sedge. The clothes are loose and don't impede the action of the limbs and are strong beside, and also have the merit of being cheap as a suit complete, hat and all can be bought at any slop-shop for $10 or less. The Sou-wester or hat is admirably adapted to the purpose, as it has a long flap behind which falls over the back and is tied under the arms, preventing effectually any water trickling down the back of your neck. A good muffler, a pair of high rubber boots with leggins attached, costing $7 ; a pair of long yarn stockings, and an old buffalo skin, or an army blanket, made of india rubber, to sit upon, will complete your outfit. If you should be going to any unfrequented place, a pound of candles, a few boxes of matches, a couple of pounds of ground coffee, a pound of tea and a little crushed sugar will help you out very materially.

BAY SNIPE SHOOTING.

A very ancient and distinguished authority upon the art of cooking, one Mrs. Glass, a lady well known and highly esteemed by your great grandmother, observes, in her treatise, that you must *first* catch your rabbit and then cook it, so you my Boys must not think, because you have your gun and shooting rig complete, you are going to bag your birds without learning to shoot them, hence you will naturally ask, where is the best place to learn and at what game? In my estimation there is no better practice for the beginner than that afforded by Bay Snipe. You may hunt quail or woodcock the day long and not get a shot, and pigeon shooting from a trap is rather too expensive for beginners, but in the months of August and September, along the shores of any of our great bays, from Montauk Point to the Chesapeake, there is not a day or an hour when the beginner may not find practice, —during that time the meadows are alive with the smaller varieties and the sand snipe fly up and down the beach in myriads. As he gains

confidence in himself he can take his seat in a
blind and try his hand at the larger varieties.
Montauk Point, Chinekok Bay, Quogue, South
Oyster Bay, Far Rockaway, are all famous for
their snipe flats, and bay-men can always be had
to take one to the shooting ground, set out his
decoys, whistle down the birds, and to direct the
tyro how to and when to shoot. These men are
all capital marksmen, inimitable in their imitation of the peculiar notes of the different birds
and thoroughly reliable, and as they furnish boat
and decoys, their charge of $2.50 per day is not
exorbitant. My advice to a beginner then would
be to go (if living in New York), to Great South
Bay, or to Barnegat Bay, early in August, and if
he can afford it, to hire one of these men, and
go out with him every day, and follow his advice
implicitly, as to the manner of holding his gun
and shooting, and at the end of the month, I confidently assert that he will know more about
gunning than many an amateur who thinks himself a sportsman. The very air of the gunning
house where he would put up, is redolent of guns
and sporting, and an attentive ear will drink in
and profit by an immense amount of information
pertaining thereto, in a month's residence among
them. If a young man is limited as to means,

there is no necessity of employing a gunner, as stools and blinds are furnished at Barnegat Bay, without charge; he can, under these circumstances, rely upon himself, and make experience his teacher. Some boys are foolishly sensitive about letting people see them, when undertaking anything for the first time. This need not deter you down at Barnegat, for you may pop away the live-long day, and not a soul will be the wiser or be within the sound of your gun.

After trying your hand at Beach Snipe, setting and flying, and becoming satisfied that you know how to hold your gun right, you can take a shot at a gull, as he sails past you, and if you miss him twenty more will pass within shot in an hour.

After a boy has knocked over a few birds on the wing, he begins to feel a confidence in himself which is very advantageous to his shooting, rendering him cooler and more observant of the causes which have led to his improvement, what birds are in range and which are not; the great difficulty, however, which he has to overcome is a reluctance to fire at a bird unless he feels certain that it is within range, and that he can bring him down; the only way is to let drive at everything that comes along where there is a

possibility of killing, for many a man misses
making a bag by waiting for birds to come nearer,
only letting them pass because he is doubtful as
to their being in range.

Before going down to Barnegat, Boys, suppose
you read the following article, which I wrote for
Wilkes' Spirit of the Times, and which was published under date of August 7, 1869, descriptive
of Sport in the Bay. It will give you an idea of
the locality and how the shooting is done there.
The article is entitled—

Snipe Shooting and Fishing in Barnegat Bay.

Dear Spirit: On a wretchedly hot day a
fortnight since, returning home from business, I
found my wife fagged and wearied, with a rue-
fully woe-begone countenance, and on asking the
whys and wherefores I was informed that " Baby
was drooping, had the summer complaint, and
must be taken to the sea-shore." The various
localities were duly discussed: Long Branch too
fashionable and too expensive; Newport and Cape
May too ditto and too far; farm cottages by the
sea stupid and uncomfortable; finally, in despair,
I suggested Barnegat Bay! Daniel Webster,
after his most magnificent effort, was never
greeted with such applause as was elicited by

that single word, Barnegat! Wife, boys and girls fairly shouted with delight, and the house shook with echoes of "Hurrah for Barnegat!" Now, be it known that for years it has been my habit to make semi-annual pilgrimages to Squam Beach in search of game, and I have always come back with a goodly bag of ducks and geese, and on each occasion a solemn promise has been exacted to take the whole kit and crew down with me some time or other — and now that time had come and there was "no going back" on them.

One day's notice was sufficient, and in twenty-four hours we were all ensconced on board the *Jessie Hoyt*, steaming down the bay to make connection with the Delaware and Raritan Bay Railroad, ticketed through to Point Pleasant. Arriving at Farmingdale, we took stage to Charley Maxon's at Point Pleasant, at the head of Barnegat Bay, and from thence, after an hour's drive along the beach, with the ocean on the one hand and bay on the other, we pulled up at Billy Chadwick's gunning-house, in just eight hours from New York. Now, for the benefit of the uninitiated, I must mention that Squam Beach is a narrow sand-pit, separated from the mainland by Barnegat Bay, having an average width of five or six hundred yards, and extending from Point Pleasant on the north down as far as the Delaware breakwater; and along its length are scattered, at intervals, houses owned by wreckers, and answering as houses of entertainment for gunners. The bay swarms with ducks and geese during fall and spring, and with snipe in summer; besides offering as fine fishing as is to be found in the world for bluefish, bass and sheepshead. Thus there is scarcely a month in the year in which the votary of gun or rod may not find enjoyment. Now Billy Chadwick's, situated seven miles from the head of the bay, is the best conducted of these houses, and may be reached from Point Pleasant by land or by one hour's sail *via* Tom's River; and having been the resort for thirty years of gentlemen sportsmen of the old school, who, while willing to rough it, *would* have things nice and clean—consequently, while the house is entirely unpretentious, it is far superior in point of comfort to the huge caravanseries at Long Branch or Cape May. Cleanliness is Madame Chadwick's first law, seconded by good coffee, good sugar, good tea, rich cream, and exquisitely cooked game, whether of fish or feather; no fuss, no obsequiousness, and egregiously small bills—*footed* up in Billy's *head*. (He keeps no accounts, save five and tally.) To this place, on a lovely summer afternoon, I drove up with wife, five children and nurse; and if the gates of heaven had opened to them there could not have been five happier faces; and even poor baby drew long breaths, as if unconsciously consuming as much as possible of the pure atmospheric food. I must own that I had felt some doubts as to my reception with such a caravan, for Billy's wife had often said she didn't mind how many gunners came, but she didn't want women around. But my doubts were quickly dispelled in the warm welcome accorded, and to my astonishment found that Billy had made an addition of a three-story verandah to his house, and that our rooms (four adjoining, with a south-easterly exposure commanding both sea and bay) were as comfortable as could be wished; and as the children tumbled into bed they dropped off to sleep, counting on their fingers the intervals between the flashes of the Barnegat light, as it burst forth and disappeared, almost eclipsed by the magnificent moon, silvering impartially bay and ocean.

Although I well knew that there was no better snipe-shooting to be found than on Billy's flat, I had no idea that so early in the season there

would be any flight; hence had simply brought
my gun as a matter of habit. Fancy my delight,
then, when I found the snipe had already appeared, and that the prospects for sport were
never brighter. Leaving the youngsters dreaming of prospective fun in their moonlit chambers,
with a gentle southeaster playing through their
curls, I went down to ask Billy more particularly
about the snipe and the morrow's shooting.
Now, Billy's big house had made him proud, so
he utterly refused to talk snipe till I had "jined
him in a glass of bourbon bought of Uncle Gilly
Davis fourteen years ago." Having taken the
medicine kindly, Billy proceeded in this wise, in
a roaring monotone:

"Now, Captain, if Providence had laid a telegraph down from the moon [Billy being a wrecker,
and consequently a moon-worshiper, always lo-
cates his elysium *there*] to your house, and sent
you a special dispatch, you couldn't hit it better.
Them yelpers keep a whistlin' and shaking their
yaller legs from daylight to dark. Marlin were
never more plenty; jack-curlews ain't so plenty;
but there is a flight of sickle-bills, and the doe-
witches and robin-snipe are as thick as flies
around a sugar-bowl."

"By the way, Bill,—excuse my interrupting

you—tell me how many blinds you have, and where they are."

Well, let me see, there's the inner and outer blind on the flat in front of the house; then there's a couple down in Nigger-house Cove, and two up in front of Uncle Sammy Chadwick's—and we can rig a dozen more if they are wanted. Now, if the wind holds where it is, I'd take the inner stand to-morrow; but if it breezes up and blows from southwest, the outer one will kill more big birds; if it hauls more to eastward, Nigger-house will be good; but if it should bear off northward, then Uncle Sammy's will be good as any, for there won't be much shootin' done anywhere."

" Good night, Billy;" and in ten minutes, after having uncased my gun, filled pouch and flask, and taken out a pair of hole-y shoes and old pants and flannel shirt, I was sound asleep. It seemed as if I had hardly got asleep when I heard a tap at the door: " Ten minutes to four, Sir!" "All right!" On go the old clothes, hole-y shoes and straw hat, and my toilet is complete; when, hastily snatching up gun and accoutrements, I sally forth, and step out into the early dawn struggling with the full moon. The air was cool and bracing, the sharp cracking of the surf

3

on the one hand contrasting with the scarcely
ruffled water of the bay, barely one hundred
yards apart. A fast step across a wet meadow,
a moment's wade across the shoal, and I found
myself in the inner blind, formed of brush breast
high, with an old cane sofa—the spoil of some
wrecked vessel—for a seat, and a shelf in front
for the ammunition. Hastily picking up a dozen
decoys and placing them within twenty yards of
the stand, I took my seat, fresh capped my gun,
and, like St. Paul when he was cast away,
waited for day and for—game. And it was not
long coming, either; for a black duck whizzed
past at about fifty yards, receiving a salute from
my two barrels, but the number eight shot never
fazed him. Not so a bunch of doe-witches, which
came skirling over the meadows, readily answering my call and circling around twice, finally
doubled over the stool, only to depart as mourn-
ers, leaving half a dozen of their number dead
among the deceitful decoys. Next came an old
jack-curlew, who evidently knew the ropes; for,
coolly gazing at the stools, then making three
successive whirls and drawing the contents of
two barrels, he finally sailed off. A flock of
marlin came manfully to stool, but, without stop-
ing to bury their dead, darted away to seek con-

solation among the decoys of the outer stand, where the balance of them terminated their career. Many a yellow-leg and creaker shared their sad fate, and by seven o'clock, in spite of many a villainous miss (of course attributable to our gun), we had a bag of twenty birds; so, leaving guns in the stand, we cheerfully responded to the breakfast bell. Assembled on the piazza, I found my mosquito fleet, who, accompanied by mamma, had been watching for some time our sport, but who were now clamorous for breakfast—and such a feed! Madam Chadwick, under the tuition of many an epicurean sportsman, not least among whom was Uncle Gilly Davis, can make a good cup of coffee, poach an egg, broil a sheepshead, or roast a snipe in a way that would do credit to Guy or Downing.

After breakfast, my little ones sued out a *habeas corpus* and obtain possession of my person, mamma being frantic with their appeals as to fishing, swimming, crabbing and sailing ; and even baby, who improves by the hour, begs to be taken down to the " big waatah." Hastily providing the bigger ones with hook and line and showing them where they could catch sunfish and perch as fast as they could bait, and

escorting mamma, baby and nurse to the beach,
adjusting shawls and parasols, and marking out
a line of sand fortifications to be at once com-
menced, I left them, to wade off again to the
blind, and barely was seated when I heard the
peculiar call of the sickle-bill. Now, the sickle-
bill is as large as a teal-duck, and, as they stool
well, offer good sport. Our answering call at-
tracted their attention, for they hesitate in their
flight, diverge, and then swoop directly for the
stool; again rise, circle twice, and then double
in front. Springing to our feet, we give them
four barrels; two—four—six are struggling
among the stool, and the rest, panic stricken
and with startled cry, hover with impunity over
our discharged guns. Oh! for a breech-loader!

Then come bunches of doe-witches, and single
birds, yellow-legs, and the rest. Though we do
some bad shooting, still by one o'clock we are
well satisfied. The dinner-bell now rings, and
papa's whistle calls together his little flock, who,
with bared feet and sun-burnt faces, are chock-
full of fishing exploits.

After dinner, lighting a cigar, we stroll over
to the government station-house, accompanied
by Billy, who has charge and keeps everything
in apple-pie order. He explains to the wife and

little ones the uses of the various implements for life-saving—the mortar, the rockets, the life-car, the great surf-boat, etc., illustrated by sundry incidents of his experience, of deadly despair succeeded by joy at being saved, of tragic deaths, of wives and husbands washed ashore stark and stiff, clinging in each others' arms even in death; then, after a swim, we go back to our stand till the sun sets; and then, thoroughly pleased with our day's sport, we lift our decoy, and go again to the house in response to the tea-bell. Now the fishing boats come dropping in, with various experiences of sheepsheading and blue-fishing and double-reefed breezes, and new comers arrive from the main with late New York papers and eager for the morrow's sport. It was a week of days like the one described, the birds coming in thicker and thicker, varied by fishing and delightful cruises in the bay, generally with Captain Gulick in his well appointed, staunch and stiff little yacht *Zouave*, or with Johnny Chadwick, or with Charley Stout, all of whom know, as if by intuition, the whereabouts and habits of fish and fowl.

One morning a fog-bank suddenly rolled in from the southward and hovered for several hours over the sea and bay; toward afternoon the breeze freshened, and as we looked over the beach we descried a vessel ashore. Hailing the house at the top of our lungs, we shouted "A wreck! a wreck!" and in two minutes every man, woman and child were streaming toward the beach, ourselves among the first. As we approached, we saw a schooner's spars looming up through the fog, close on to the beach, and, hailing her, found her the *R. J. Whillden*, of Philadelphia, wanting assistance. Billy being sub-agent for the Coast Wrecking Company, dispatched a man on horseback to the nearest telegraph station; while our services as a sea-faring man were enlisted to draw up contracts, and in twelve hours the Company's steamers *Relief* and *Winan* were alongside, and all appliances necessary for hauling her off put into requisition. The children were frantic with delight, as a wreck had never been even dreamed of in their programme.

And now, dear SPIRIT, if any of your readers want a few days' good sport, let me recommend them to do as I did. They can take the *Jessie Hoyt* at 4 p. m., buy a ticket on board for Tom's River, arriving about eight, take the *Zouave* across the bay, and sleep snugly at Billy Chadwick's, in readiness for the next day's sport.

The foregoing is one of several articles written by me for sporting papers, three of which I propose to introduce here as descriptive of Fishing, Shooting and Sailing in Barnegat Bay, and are reliable so far as to convey a correct idea of the game and mode of pursuing it.

Now, then, imagine yourselves in a blind set up on a sand-flat where the water is two or three feet deep, and some twenty or thirty decoys representing half a dozen varieties of snipe arranged in semi-circular rows, the outer row being at a distance of say twenty-five yards. The blind is made of bushes about four feet in height, stuck into the sand in a circular form, the area of the circle being sufficiently large to hold three men comfortably. Inside the blind a cane settee (when you can get it), or a seat made by driving down two uprights with a plank nailed across them, and also a similar contrivance a little more elevated, which is placed in front of the seat for a shelf for guns to lean against, and whereon to place the ammunition. Here we are, then, loaded up with 3 drams of powder and $1\frac{1}{4}$ ounce of No. 8 shot, the day is just breaking, and the bay rippled by a pleasant breeze blowing from the southard, which, as our stand faces to the

northard, and these birds always fly to windward, is just what we want. Our attention,
which had been diverted by quantities of crabs
circulating about our feet, which are hanging
in the water, is suddenly aroused by a sharp
musical whistle. Ha! what's that? The sound
is unmistakable, the gunner may approximate
nearly but can never exactly imitate it; there is
a metallic ring to it which nothing but the throat
of the snipe can produce, but our imitation is
sufficient for the purpose of calling the birds
and we soon receive a response to our call, and
presently descry a large bunch of snipe heading
up over the meadow for our stand. Stoop low,
boys, and don't move your head above the
bushes, and pay attention to note of bird in order that you can counterfeit it. Now, then,
cock your gun; you, Jack, take them on the left
hand as they fly past; and you, Schuyler, let
drive at anything in front of you, but be sure in
your excitement you don't shoot across our
faces. Now, then, keep cool, don't fire till I say
the word. Now, then, look out, here they come!
to-weet! to-weet! Now, then! bang! bang!
bang-bang! Keep quiet, can't you? don't rush
out, they're all dead and the wind will sweep
them into the stand. Now, then, load quickly,

but keep cool. No! they can't get away, stupid.
Jack you fired too quick, and Schuyler you shot
under your bird, and don't forget that at the
flash, birds always dart upward; another thing,
always single *one particular* bird, no matter if
there are five hundred, for birds are never so
close together as they seem. Are you loaded?
all right! You, Jack, wade out and pick up
those birds. Eight—nine; there are two more
off to the right; there's one more; there's another—thirteen, ain't there? What kind are
these, dad? They are big yellow-legs—they call
them yelpers down here, I believe. Now then,
Jack, pull the longest feather you can get from
their wing and string them by running the end of
the quill through that little hole in their bill—so;
bunch them in half dozens and hang them in the
shade, for they won't keep in this hot sun. Don't
put them in the water, for the crabs will walk off
with them. What a pity we didn't bring some
pulverized charcoal, a little of that thrust down
their throats would keep them from spoiling.

What are those? Why, they are sand snipe.
Good to eat? Yes, regular little butter balls, but
they are not worth cooking unless you get three
or four dozen, as one only makes a mouthful.
See, there are at least a hundred, and here they

3*

come. Now you, Schuyler, watch your chance when they double, aim at one in the centre and give them both barrels. Good for you! Why it looked like a snow storm. You peppered them well, there must be twenty or thirty down. Load up now, for I see a big bunch of doe-witches skirling around the other stand; lie low; how pretty they come. Now, Schuyler, wait till I give the word. Now, then! bang, bang! here they come round again—bang! What! only five? Sweet, pretty birds, aren't they? Why they look just like woodcock. They must be a cross between woodcock and English snipe. How far their eyes are set back. Pretty plumage, isn't it?

Quiet! down with you, hear those sickle-bills. Now don't move; hear how different their call is from that of the yellow-leg, and how much more difficult to imitate. Here they come, they're pretty high though. How big they look. Here they come sure enough; now each pick out one, remember, and don't fire too quick. Now, then, fire! Well, we got four, anyhow. Run out and get that fellow, Jack, he is only wing-broke. Beautiful plumage, isn't it? What a pretty contrast the white and deep brown feathers make. That fellow's bill is at least eight inches long—he's a whopper.

Now it's breezing up from southard and they'll
fly lower. Jack, wade out there and try your
hand on that old yellow-leg stalking along. Take
your time, keep to leeward of him, walk slow,
I'll hold up my handkerchief when you're near
enough to shoot. Missed him, by ginger! downed
him with the other barrel. Good boy, go up
head; you over-shot him, Jack, with your first
barrel, I saw the shot furrow up the sand beyond
him. Down close now, here comes a jack-curlew,
he will give us a shot; let me take him though.
Now watch as I shoot; he won't stool, I see that,
but see how he is coming; now I'll point at least
three feet ahead of him — bang! pick him up,
Skile. You see he is a big fellow, but his bill is
not curved like the sickle-bill, and it is not nearly
so long; not over three inches, I should say.

Father, how many varieties of snipe are there
in all conscience? I believe there are reckoned
to be at least twenty-eight different varieties.
Twenty-eight! Yes, so the naturalists say, but
if we were to shoot the whole season we probably
should not get over a dozen different varieties.

Do you ever shoot the golden plover down
here? Yes, but not a great many; they are shot
in enormous quantities about Montauk Point, arriving there in latter part of August. What do

they call them golden for? Because, although the general color is green, still they are marked with yellowish spots almost golden, so bright are they. I have seen them shot off Bill's piazza. Then there's the upland plover, they are very wild. We used to shoot them on Hempstead Plains out of a wagon, as it was impossible to get near them on foot. They are very much prized by epicures. They are also shot from behind blinds in the fields, and can be readily called by an experienced whistler.

See that flock, they're big birds, and coming this way, too, father. Yes, yes; I see them, they're willets, sure as you're born. Hark! what a sharp, thick whistle they have. Do you hear them answering our call? They'll come good, only keep quiet. Don't be sticking your gun barrel up in the sun like that. Now you've got it down in the sand, you *couldn't do a more dangerous thing;* if you had fired it off with that wad of sand in it, it would have burst to a certainty; never forget that, either of you. Here they come! Now, then, give it to them. Five down. Now load up quick as you can, I'll pick them up. Did you ever see a prettier bird, they are big fellows, too. What a pretty contrast between the white and black feathers, and how tame they were; did you see how they came back after we had fired—that was the time for a breech-loader.

What are those coming, doe-witches? No, robin snipe, and they're coming right at us, too. Bang, bang! ten down as I'm a sinner; the whole crowd wanted to light and would have done so if we had let them. They do look like a robin, don't they? and for the table they are as delicious as any snipe that flies over the bay.

How hot the water feels, its really disagreeable to the feet, and if they were bare the sun would blister them, so you see its a great deal better to wear a pair of hole-y shoes and thin pants, for you thus avoid the crabs and clam shells and old bottle necks. Father I would like to stay here all summer and come to this blind every day; why it's as good as a picture to see all these schooners working down the beach, and those ships standing off, and all those boats passing in and out, to and from Bill's house. There comes Capt. Hat. Gulick over from the main. I hope there ain't any more snipe shooters aboard, we're full enough at the house already, and blessed if there ain't Charley Stout, too, with a load of clams in the old "Hickory"—they say she's fifty years old if she's a day.

What's that Bill's waving to us about. Why, look there, there are about fifty marlin going to the other stand and there's no one in it. Keep down now. Cock your guns, but don't shoot one second before I tell you to. Here they come, jimmencty! they're as big as ducks. Shoo! quiet! Now, then, bang! bang! bang! Five — six — seven, by all that's lovely! Pick 'em up, boys, for I hear the dinner-bell. Now, then, gather up your birds; hold your guns high up so the water won't splash; come along, we have had one good day, anyhow.

This is a pretty good wade, boys, look out for your guns, don't stumble. Hullo! here comes Bill to meet us. Well, boys, "you have everlastingly rattled them" to-day, sure enough, your stand was like Fort Sumter. Who was it that shot that single jack? he was everlastingly a bilin' along. Now, then, hurry up, boys, if you're going to take a swim, for supper will be ready in half an hour.

So off we put for the surf, and a good supper and a good smoke for papa ends the day.

ENGLISH SNIPE.

When I was a lad, Mr. Henry William Herbert, so well known as Frank Forrester, as accomplished a sportsman and gentleman as ever lived, gave lessons in a school where I was being educated, and of course the big boys used occasionally, when he was in a good humor, beguile him into converse upon sporting matters; and although not in that category (not being a big boy) myself, still I used to listen with avidity, and I well remember hearing him say: "Boys, the most difficult bird to shoot in America is the English snipe, and when you can knock over your two birds right and left you may consider yourself a good shot;" and he never said a truer word, for a successful snipe shot must be considered a good shot anywhere. This bird may be ranked second to no game bird in America, both for the sport he affords, as well as for the table, for no more delicious morsel tempts the palate of the epicure; yet, strange to say, although so highly appreciated, they are more plentiful the country over than any bird that flies. North, south, east and west, wherever there are stretches of meadow

land along our river bottoms, along our great
lakes and the ocean, they periodically appear.
They breed in Labrador and appear during the
late spring months with their young on the flats
in the vicinity of the St. Lawrence, where they are
shot in large numbers, as well as along the northern lakes, gradually working their way to the
south, reaching us here late in September, and
remaining with us until the early frost, and then
move off to the far south, where they literally
swarm during the winter months. They are an
extremely erratic and uncertain bird to find; one
day they will be seen in large quantities feeding
on a neighboring meadow, the next there will not
one be found. Being exceedingly sensitive to
changes of temperature, a blustering day or two
will be sufficient to effect an entire change of
base; or a heavy tide, over-running their feeding
ground, will frequently disperse them. In our
district of country, say within an area of 200
miles around New York, the English snipe makes
his appearance somewhere from 20th March to
15th April, according to the season, for the frost
must be sufficiently out of the ground to enable
him to bore for his food—worms, larvæ of in-
sects, roots of tender aquatic plants, etc., etc.—
they are then migrating towards the north for the

purpose of incubation, and besides being exceedingly shy, they stay but a short time. Perhaps the best day to choose for a snipe shoot is after a long north-easterly storm on a balmy day in April, but the spring birds after all are shy and thin and do not afford any very great sport. They reappear, however, in September and October, when they are in good condition, and they then lay better to the dogs and it's much more satisfactory sport. The hunting of these birds involves an enormous deal of fatigue, as they lie hidden in treacherous morasses, every step through which frequently brings the sportsman knee deep, and often waist deep, in the mud and mire, and the mere physical exertion necessary to get over a few miles of such ground is apt, and undoubtedly does, much towards unsettling a man's nerves and interferes with his shooting. Independently of all else, no birds lie so closely as do these snipe, and hidden, as they are, under tussocks of grass, it requires a keen scent to find them, frequently permitting the dogs to run over them before they will get up; and when they rise they do it with such lightning swiftness and on such an eccentric zig-zag that it requires long practice to kill them, and an expert marker to mark them down. The usual dodge, so far as I can judge, is to dart up breast high and then to shoot off either to the right or left like lightning, and appearing so small a mark it requires considerable skill to cover them; indeed, a man who can, on such an unstable foundation, and after floundering and plunging about in a hot sun for hours on a wet meadow, a man, I say, who can, under such circumstances, with any certainty kill his double birds may not be ashamed of his shooting.

In former years those extensive flats known as the Newark and Paterson Meadows, used to be a favorite feeding ground, and being easy of access to New York, a lively fusilade was carried on from the time of their appearance until their disappearance; but, from what I can learn, such constant shooting has had the effect of driving them to more secluded feeding grounds, although a moderate day's sport may still be enjoyed in these localities. The meadows along the Raritan and Delaware Rivers still attract them, and being accessible afford the means of enjoyment to many sportsmen from New York and Philadelphia; but if any one wants a real good day's sport let me recommend him to go to " Point Pleasant," at the northern extremity of Barnegat Bay (accessible by rail from New York in three hours' time), and securing the services of as fine a shot as ever fired a gun, Jimmy Loveman, take a tramp over the neighboring meadows—a line addressed to Jimmy will secure an immediate reply as to proper time to go, etc., etc. Jimmy has good dogs always, and dogs broken on snipe, which is to the last degree important, for otherwise a dog, however good his pedigree, and however keen his nose, and excellent though he may be on woodcock, for English snipe he is good for nothing; indeed, excepting for retrieving purposes on a meadow where snipe are plenty, I would rather be without a dog than with one, provided I am not entirely assured of his proficiency in this respect, having had several days' shooting spoiled by woodcock and quail dogs, whose owner insisted upon bringing them, acting upon the theory that a good dog, well broken, is good for every kind of game.

For autumn snipe shooting a man wants as light a rig as possible, for, although the mornings and evenings are cool, a September or October sun is hot, and where a man has to haul either leg out of two or three feet of sticky mire every time he steps he wants as little clothing as possible, a light gun and as little ammunition as he can manage to make out with. A sharp

shooting No. 12 gun, weighing 7½ lbs., shooting
2½ drams of powder and an ounce of No. 8 shot,
is about the ticket. If you have to drive any
distance a heavy overcoat is good for morning
and evening, and especially after the day's exercise. For autumn shooting I should recommend
a pair of very thin hole-y boots over light woolen
socks, the pantaloon tied around the ankle; but
for spring shooting, where the water is icy cold,
one wants a pair of high boots with leggins attached, and flannel under clothing.

If I attempted to give a disquisition upon the
peculiar habits of the snipe I might write half a
dozen chapters, but it would be entirely out of
place here, and I will simply say that you must
not let the idea run away with you that they confine themselves entirely to wet, for its a great
mistake so to suppose; on the contrary, when
the tides are very high and cover the meadows,
they will retreat to fields at a considerable distance, and, under those circumstances, I have
put them up from corn fields and upland meadows
in considerable numbers.

Chadwick's Gunning House, Squam Beach.

(As it was before it was rebuilt two years ago.)

DUCKING.

Give me duck shooting, I say, above all other. It's all very fine to shoot at a deer, but it is not so fine to be backed up against a pine tree for half a dozen hours waiting for him to come, and when he does ten to one you won't be ready for him and will miss him. No! no! I say there is no sport that is accessible to us denizens of cities so exciting as duck and goose shooting. The charm consists, perhaps, not so much in bringing down the game as in the surroundings; the total and absolute change from the conventionalism of city life, involving as it does, as a general thing, what is usually considered great hardship and exposure, but which in reality is the charm of the expedition. To a man who has been caged for months in an office, reduced to a mere machine, run for the purpose of turning out so many dollars per diem, whose only exercise has been an occasional walk of a mile, or so, between his luxurious residence and his place of business, the change to a fisherman's hovel on an open beach, with a snow storm driving through its every crack and cranny, could hardly be more radical; accustomed to extreme city hours, the pillow at eight p.m., and the reveillé at three a. m., must be startling. A four miles' sail in a sneak "box" to his shooting point, before dawn, and a day passed in recumbent position, on a wet meadow, all this, it must be confessed, must seem novel, yet there *is* an indescribable something about it which yearly attracts men of refinement and means, who at home enjoy every luxury which money can bestow; to me it is irresistible. The sail across the bay, of an autumnal night, under a close-reefed sail, with a nor'easter howling about us; the arrival and honest shake of the rough hand; the thundering breaker bursting on the beach; the welcome supper; the pipe in the smoky bar, the night-cap of mountain dew, the old fashioned feather bed, with the gale driving the snow in upon you, and the roar of the surf as a lullaby; the flaring candle in your eyes, summoning you to get up; the steaming breakfast, partaken by a dozen men in full hunting costume; the exit into the frosty air of a November night, for night it is yet and will be for two hours; the sail across the bay to your point, in the silent watches of the night. Reaching the point, the reconstruction of the nest or blind, the adjustment of water-proof, then the eager waiting for day and game, the "honk" of the gunner, as a bunch of black duck come winding round the point, scarce discernible in the gloaming; the admonitory "get ready," the half-cock of the gun, the bang! bang! bang! the splash of the game in the water, all! all! carries with it a fascination too irresistible to be analysed on rationalistic grounds. I will tell you what it is. It is manhood asserting its dignity! Shut up in offices, or dens rather, of law or of commerce, climbing a daily treadmill, slaves to our customers or our clients, we inwardly feel a contempt for ourselves, and oftentimes an abhorrence for our calling and those whose patronage gives us our bread and butter; to such this life is a safety valve. * * *

As the strong nor'easter sweeps across the bay, we spring forward and lend a hand at reefing; a bunch of geese come to our stand, we snatch our No. 6 gun and bring half-a-dozen floundering to the water; a vessel comes ashore and we volunteer our services to board her. What is the motive which prompts to all this seeming sacrifice? Simply and only a desire to convince ourselves that " a mon's a mon for a' that."

The autumnal ducking season sets in in September and continues until cold weather, and is enjoyed all along the shores of the Eastern States, through the Vineyard Sounds, at Montauk Point, Chinekok Bay, Great South Bay, Oyster Bay, Jamaica Bay, Barnegat Bay, the Chesapeake, and the sounds along the seaboard of the Southern States. Those living in New York may, in four or five hours, reach the localities by taking the Long Island road for the points on Great South Bay, Chinekok Bay, or South Oyster Bay, or by the Jersey Southern Railway to Barnegat Bay. There is but little doubt, however, that the fall shooting, in these localities, is over done, and that he who has the means to go to Currituck will enjoy better shooting there. In the vicinity of Norfolk even, (without going so far as Currituck,) at Cherrystone and other places, the fowling is especially fine, a party of four friends of mine having bagged, last year, within a week, over two hundred head of geese and brant. Currituck, although on the coast of North Carolina, is not inaccessible, for one can leave the foot of Cortlandt street at 8.45 a. m., arrive at Norfolk next morning; take propeller, which connects through the Dismal Swamp, and be on his ground before evening, stay ten days, and his trip will not necessarily cost him over a hundred

dollars. I have before told you that for duck
shooting you want all your wrappers and water-
proofs and long India rubber boots, a gun heavy
in the breech, say a No. 8 guage, charged with
five drams of Curtis & Harvey powder and
two ounces No. 4 shot, if shooting ducks alone,
but if there is a chance for geese, the second
barrel should be loaded with double B's, *though*,
of course, if you shoot a breech-loader, you can
shift your charge at pleasure. None but those
who have witnessed it, can conceive of the vast
number of ducks and geese that congregate in
the bays above mentioned. They can often be
computed by the tens of thousands, and yet it
not unfrequently occurs that when the largest
number is in the bay the shooting is most
indifferent; this is easily accounted for, in-
asmuch as it is only in boisterous weather that
the fowl leave their feeding ground and fly off
from point to point; hence the best time to go
to those places is after a heavy gale of wind,
which generally raises a sea in the bays and the
tide also, which routs the fowl up so that
they keep on the wing. The best time, in my
opinion, to go to Long Island, in the autumn,
for ducks and geese (in the average season)
is the 1st November; to the upper end of

4

Barnegat Bay, about the same time, but down below the inlet, the 15th of the month is early enough, and to Norfolk or Currituck a month later.

For the spring shooting one must be governed entirely by the season, but as soon as he hears that the bays are free from ice, he may go down with impunity. I have shot off Northwest Point, in upper end of Barnegat Bay, as early as 22d February, but as a general thing the 20th March is quite early enough. The spring shooting is by far the finest, and the game much more abundant. Immense numbers of geese were killed at South Oyster Bay, last spring, as late as middle of April, and I never saw such vast flocks of brant as were congregated about the inlet of Barnegat Bay, at the same time.

The varieties of ducks that we usually shoot in this section of country are the black duck, widgeon, sprigtail, green and blue-winged teal, the spoon-bill, canvas-back, red-head, broad-bill, whistler, dipper, old wife, and shell-drake; we also shoot the brant and Canada geese in large quantities, but only occasionally a swan. Indeed, I have in one day's shooting, in Barnegat Bay, shot at all these varieties.

Duck and goose shooting from points is not disagreeable, as one can move about when the game is not flying thick, and he can always keep out of the wind, and generally manage to keep warm, but in shooting out of boats he is obliged to lie the greater part of the time, as if he were in his coffin, without moving a muscle, the consequence is that he is cramped and stiff to the last degree, and, if unaccustomed to it, is in no condition to shoot, and rarely does any execution at the first. Indeed a man, to be a good shot at ducks, must have had experience, for not only the recumbent position and the heavy wrappings, but the lightning speed of the birds and their peculiar gyrations upset his calculations and he will inevitably, for a time, shoot behind them and frequently above them, as these birds will jump at the flash and climb into the air with miraculous velocity. As the usual flight of these birds is sixty miles per hour and when disturbed reaches ninety miles, it is very easy to shoot behind them, indeed by no possibility can they be hit unless the gun is aimed at least one foot ahead of them.

In point of numbers, the quantity of wild fowl that pass and repass our bays and estuaries, each fall and spring, is simply inconceivable.

I have seen them feeding, acres on acres of them, and when they rose it was like distant thunder, and like a huge curtain spread before the sun ; and remember an occasion, sitting on the beach, on a soft balmy day in November, from early in the morning until night, and scarcely seeing a break in the continuous line of ducks, geese and brant, bound south. How many fowl passed in those seven or eight hours it would be a difficult matter to compute.

DUCK SHOOTING IN BARNEGAT BAY.

"Written by me for *Wilkes' Spirit of the Times*," Nov. 19, 1864.

Last week, having a little spare time on our hands, we resolved to go down to Barnegat Bay and have a shot at the ducks, and we accordingly duly announced our intention in family council, whereupon our better half immediately had a vision of a week's rollicking, unbecoming a pater-familias, to be followed by a sharp attack of inflammatory rheumatism. The youngsters, however, received the announcement with demonstrations of evident delight, as being suggestive of long stories for approaching winter's entertainments, and forthwith began to "quack" and "honk," in the most deafening

manner, and frantic rushes were made for our
boots, over-alls and shooting equipments generally. No. 4, whom we call the General, in his
military capacity, seized our gun; No. 3, who,
judging from her pugnacious disposition, will
be a second Joan d'Arc, joining issue for its possession, while No. 2, rejoicing in the name of
Schuyler, and true to his historic antecedents,
was bestowing his attention upon the ammunition, and No. 1, (our John,) quietly assumed the
post of Inspector-General and issued his orders
with great dignity. Our preparations made, we
proceeded to the steamboat, but found to our
consternation, shared by some twenty sportsmen,
that she was incapacitated and could not leave.
An hour of awful suspense elapsed, setters and
pointers gave forth low growls of dissatisfaction,
and gunners, after staring each other in the
face and out of countenance, gradually, under
the influence of case bottles, grew friendly and
breathed vows of vengeance against steamers
generally. A substitute was, however, finally
furnished, when, shifting our traps, we were soon
steaming down the bay, and a picturesque group
we formed, in our gunning costumes, with half-
a-dozen thoughtful dogs artistically interspersed
among us. Away we whisked down the bay, pass-

ing Owl's Head, Lafayette, through the Swash Channel to Port Monmouth, and thence by rail and stage to Tom's River, where, having had a capital feed, we got aboard the little "Zouave," and stretched across the bay to Bill Chadwick's. "Quango," the great Newfoundland, saluting us as we touch the beach, accompanied us to the house, where we found a "goodlie" company of gunners assembled.

The little low bar-room looked cosily familiar to us, as we peered through a cloud of tobacco-smoke, as did the faces of the various gunners there assembled,—Jno. Harbor, Zeph., Charley Stout, Dave, Lishe, Jno. Gaunt, and the rest of them, as they warmly welcomed us. The style of accommodation is peculiar to the beach, and gunners are generally expected to sleep double. We, ourselves, were too tired to be particular, so we turned in with our boatman, and had hardly, as we thought, got to sleep, when a candle flashed before our eyes, and a rough shake of the shoulder, brought us to the consciousness that it was three o'clock, a.m., and time to get up. Without waiting to yawn, we sprang up, and in a quarter of an hour were arrayed in full shooting costume and were sitting down to a substantial breakfast. It was still pitch dark

when we slipped into our sneak boat, nor indeed
had the day fairly broken until we were comfortably sitting in our blind, with our gun at half-
cock, waiting for a flock of ducks. By way of
digression, let us here state what is, in our opinion, an essential to the comfort of the duck
shooter. What we call blinds in the northern
part of the bay, are simply points of meadow,
jutting out into the bay, always damp and frequently very wet ; on the extreme end of these
points, a circular rampart of reeds and sea grass,
about thirty inches high is thrown up, within
which the gunners (two generally,) recline, watching their decoys, which float at anchor within
thirty yards of the point. Now as the gunner is
always exposed to the bleak winds sweeping
over the meadows, and is obliged twenty times
a day to lie flat on his back in the wet sedge, it
becomes necessary to provide the proper clothing
to guard against a thorough wetting, with its
attendants of cold and rheumatics. We therefore make the following suggestions, viz: heavy
woolen stockings and the thickest possible
woolen drawers and under-shirts, as well as a
worsted muffler for the throat, with a pair of
long loose rubber boots, and over these again an
oil-skin suit (the color of the sedge), which can

be bought at any slop shop along West street, hat and all, for $10. We should also advise an India-rubber army blanket, or a buffalo robe, and an army satchel for ammunition.

When we broke off into the foregoing digression, we were reclining on our batteries awaiting a shot. Unfortunately for us, however, the wind had been strong from northwest for six weeks past and was then blowing therefrom, the very worst possible direction, and the weather had been so mild that the ducks had hardly begun to migrate and the only ones that one could hope to get a bang at were the regular traders, who rarely came to stool, being too knowing by half. Just as day was breaking, however, half a dozen dippers came down and took a look at our stool, but seeing the point, wheeled and shot away, but took with them a couple of charges, killing two and crippling a third. Barely were we loaded again, when " quack, quack," goes the gunner, and three black ducks come sweeping along, spy the stool, give an answering " quack," but sail out of gunshot. Hardly are they gone by, when down we go again—p-r-r-r, p-r-r-r, and up come a bunch of broad-bill, and as they flutter over the stool we give them three barrels and turn them over on their backs; while loading, a flock of

mallard poise over us for an instant, answer our
"quack," but catching sight of us, are off again;
hardly are we capped before, just over the edge
of the horizon, we see a long string of geese
heading for us this time, and we as flat as pan-
cakes—(a small pool of water trickling down the
back of our necks) * * "Honk, honk" from
the stand—"honk, honk," goes goosey, and down
comes the flock within a couple of hundred yards
of the stool, then follows a long conversation
between the inmates of the stand and the different members of the flock—first, the conventional
"honk," which being politely answered is equiva-
lent to "How do you do?" "Very well, thank
you!" Then comes a low quack, quack, quack
(not unlike the enunciation of a London cabby,
on a wet night, when, in shortest and most gut-
teral tones, he compresses into the smallest possible dimensions the word cab), this last quack,
signifies walk in if you please, after which, as
goosey more nearly approaches, a dialogue in an
unknown dialect ensues between fowl and gunner,
which generally ends in the slaughter of the
victim. * * * * Hallo! here come the ducks
again, three big black ducks—quack! quack!—
bang! bang!—down go two and away swims off
the third, badly hit though.

4*

"John! how wild the birds are, don't you think they get wilder every year?" "Well, yes, in the earlier part of the season, but when the flight begins in earnest, the new comers come to stool as well as ever." "There are a good many gunning houses along the bay,— eh, John?" "Yes, coming down the beach from the point, there's Jakey's, Bill Chadwick's, Ortley's, Amos Grant's, and Martin's at the inlet, Double Jim's and Kenzie's below that, beside a score on the main, and they all have their advantages too. In the early fall, the shooting at the head of the bay is best, but toward December, when the geese and brant come, we think that Double Jim's and Kenzie's kill most; but Bill Chadwick's is a sort of inter-mediate place, embodying greater advantages than any." * * * Although we have before described Chadwick's, we will again venture a few passing words upon it.

Imagine a sand-spit betwixt bay and ocean, say eighteen hundred yards across, of glittering white sand thrown up into hummocks of all con-ceivable shapes by the autumnal gales, and mid-way between the raging surf and the waters of the bay a large, low beach-house, the roof slop-ing down to within six feet of the ground, sheltering a low corridor surrounding it, the only other building in sight of the life-boat station. Everything is suggestive of desolation as we approach, all the gunners being absent on the various points. Not a soul is to be seen, the only visible object beside the house being the debris of wrecks, here a rudder with its spokeless wheel and torn stearing gear, there a spectral looking spar, encircled by the top, looking like the cross which, in Spanish countries, is raised over the murdered man.

As we step ashore, "Quango," a Newfoundland bitch, who swam ashore from a wreck, comes down to meet us, expressing the most canine affection at our return, and as we walked into the yard everything reminds us even more forcibly of ruin and desolation; and as our eye wanders over the "head-boards" washed ashore from wrecked ships nailed along the corridor, we unconsciously read aloud the names: "Samuel Willetts," "Pilgrim," "T. Hathorn," "Darax," "Honduras"—and a husky, croaking, shaky voice at our side says: "Aye! young man, you may well speak low, you would *whisper* those names if you had see'd what I have see'd. I see'd 'em all come ashore and helped save all them as was saved, and to bury them as was dead." Heigho!

there were some fine lads amongst those fourteen men—as they lay stiff and stark on the cold
wet sand, and the "poor dear," as she stood
upon the broken deck, her hair streaming in the
wind, with her arms around her husband's neck;
and afterwards as they lay together in the clear
moonlight with faces as white as the sand about
them, and their arms, though stiff and stark, still
encircling each other. Eh! boys! you may well
look sad—you may see 'em yet in any wild night
as the moon breaks through the cloud drifts, if
you walk along the beach. But, though desolate
outside, there's no cosier place within than Bill
Chadwick's, and we defy any one to be gloomy
as he sits about the bar-room fire after the day's
sport is over, exchanging experiences, cleaning
guns, replenishing ammunition and listening to
a *Mosaic* conversation never outdone since the
building of Babel. * * * * Every gunner
has his say; every phase of duck-shooting is discussed; guns are inspected and compared, and
loud above the rest a young man is eloquent upon the beauties of Hakodadi women, appeal-
ing, in support of his assertions, to another
who had spent years in the China seas smug-
gling opium.

This polyglot is going on in an atmosphere of

tobacco smoke dense as a London fog, indeed in
that low murky room scarce six feet high from
floor to ceiling, barely lighted by a kerosene
lamp, whose flickering flames struggled with the
tobacco fumes for mastery, there was a grouping
picturesque in costume, noble in form, with surroundings of fowling gear and game that would
have delighted Vandyke or Murillo.

QUAIL.

Boys, you know almost as much about the
habits of pretty Bob White as I can teach you.
You have heard him whistling to his wife and
children so many times of a still summer day,
and hopping saucily ahead of the carriage in
the roadway, as much as to say, "it isn't November yet, and I'm all right 'till then," that
it is hardly worth my while to dwell long upon his habits, and you know too, you young
scamps, that the old lady lays a dozen prettily
speckled eggs, and that if she is not bothered
by young poachers like you, she will, after
hatching and bringing up properly her first lit-

tle family, proceed to lay, and then set and hatch them out too, and they say that she will sometimes rear a third set of children. All this, however, depends upon the season. If the spring is late and cold, she would not have time for all this; and if the early spring should be followed by wet months of May and June, the young broods will die altogether, and only the old birds will be left. It has happened in our part of the country several times, that after a very hard winter and wet spring, that the old birds have been shot off in the fall, that there have been almost none left at all; and it has been only owing to the wonderful breeding powers of the bird that it has not altogether disappeared. Heavy snow storms are very hard upon the Quail, in that it covers up all their means of subsistence, burying them at the same time; and if the top of the snow crusts with ice, the birds perish, as they cannot then force their way out. You remember, perhaps, in the fall of the year, at the beginning of cold weather, to have seen a covey of birds huddled together; you recollect they form a circle, with their heads out and tails in. In this position a snow storm often overtakes them, completely covering them up to the depth of a foot or more. If the snow does not crust, they, by their united strength, manage to lift this snow from on top of them, and fly off to neighboring barn-yards and share the food of the poultry, often becoming very tame ; but if a rain follows the snow and then a sharp frost, the snow proves their winding sheet. We fortunately live in a climate which is peculiarly favorable to them, and if they are properly protected there need be no apprehension of their extinction ; but if pot-hunters and gunners for a market, and other men who ought and do know better, insist upon shooting them all the year round, it will only require two or three hard winters and unfavorable springs to make them as scarce as the mastodon. The period allowed under Jersey law for shooting them is from the first of November until the first of January, and any one who can shoot them within that period is welcome to them, for they are in prime condition and strong of flight, and worthy of the sportsman's lead.

The universality of the quail in every country and every clime save the very cold is an astonishing thing. I myself have shot them in large numbers in Western Mexico, where the thermometer never falls below 70°, and frequently ranges at 100° to 105° Fahrenheit, and still their flesh

was as firm as if shot here. All through the
great West, and from Oregon to Sonora, on the
Pacific, these birds abound, and on the Pacific
Slope they are a positive pest to the farmer; and
even so near to us as the valley of the Ohio
River, at a point which we, living in New York,
may easily reach in twenty-four hours, these
birds are netted in enormous quantities, and unlike any other game bird, they thrive in the
presence of civilization; and, as I before remarked, were it not for the poacher and pot-
hunter, we need never want a day's sport over .
our grain stubble from November to January.

Sportsmen living in the City of New York can,
within one hour's travel on any railroad running
north, south, east or west, get upon quail ground;
but, as in the vicinity of the city land-owners are
beginning to preserve their game, one cannot well
attempt to shoot without permission, and that
permission may not be granted; therefore, any
one who could spare the time had far better go
further, with a certainty of sport as a reward for
his trouble. Southern and Eastern New Jersey
swarms with quail, and is made accessible by the
Southern Railroad of New Jersey; Pennsylvania
by the New Jersey Railroad in conjunction with
the Pennsylvania Railroad, making any small

town fifty miles west of Philadelphia a base of operations. Havre de Grasse in Maryland is a good central point from whence to diverge, or Parkersburg, Virginia, on the Baltimore and Ohio Railroad.

One great reason why quail shooting is so highly esteemed by sportsmen, is that these birds give such a capital opportunity for the display of the admirable qualities of the thorough-bred and well-trained hunting dog; in fact, it is the only shooting in this country where a dog, so to speak, can do himself justice. In woodcock shooting, in nine cases out of ten, the dog is hidden in some impenetrable swamp or cane-break, and often after standing on a bird till his patience gives out or the bird flies, he finally, in disgust, seeks his master, whose efforts to reach him have been unsuccessful. In snipe shooting the unfortunate dog is baffled in his scent by the water or the meadows, and wearied out by dragging himself through mud and mire, and pursuing birds that will not lie to his point. But in quail shooting all this is reversed; these birds love the wheat, rye and oat stubble, where the ground is hard and firm, and especially the buckwheat stubble, where they luxuriate if undisturbed; and in an open country such as Pennsylvania, where there is but little cover and the birds are not over much shot at, half a dozen bevies may often be found within an area of one hundred acres, which may be almost exterminated without leaving the open at all. Here it is that the finer qualities of thoroughly broken dogs may be seen to advantage and appreciated. How quiet they lie at your feet among the buffalo skins, their soft eyes occasionally meeting yours, as if deprecating the length of the drive; yet how they tremble in eager expectation of the sport they know that they are to participate in. How, although quivering with excitement, how obediently they come to heel and charge, while you are loading; and then, as you wave them right to left, how they shoot like lightning across the stubble field, and before the first impetus of their rush is accomplished, obedient to the first note of your whistle, how they pause in mid career, intelligently raise their heads, and then, at a second signal, quarter the ground with beautiful precision. Suddenly their speed is decreased, their movements become more guarded, their bodies quiver with intense excitement, and abruptly they stop, coming to a dead halt, and grow as stiff as pieces of statuary, the one in advance of the other. This is a sight that can only be appreciated by a sportsman, but by him it is beloved above all others.

Boys, suppose we have a day with the quails. * * * The morning is clear and frosty, the atmosphere crystalline and bracing, but a southerly wind admonishes us not to dress too heavily, or, as the sun gets higher, we shall suffer from the heat. Arrayed in corduroy, with well-fitting stout walking shoes, and a light overcoat to break the chilliness, we throw our gun cases into the wagon, and, whistling to our dogs eagerly awaiting the signal, and who, in obedience, jump in and stow themselves away without our assistance, we drive off at a brisk trot. A few miles of fine road brings us to a snug country tavern, where leaving our team, we are soon on our shooting ground, which discovers a range of several hundred acres of closely harvested grain stubble. Calling our dogs into heel, we jump a ditch, and, separating, advance abreast, waving our dogs onward. How well they know their business! how swiftly, yet how cautiously, they hunt. Toho! toho! "Shot!" good dog! careful! c-a-refully! Steady, Sport, steady, you sir! See how cat-like they approach! how they fairly quiver! how they stretch forward their necks, and bending their forelegs, almost trail their long-haired bellies on the ground.

Now, see! could carved marble be more immovable? Now, Jack, move forward a little to the right. Now, stand ready and I will flush them. Whir-r-r! whir-r-r! Bang! bang! Watch where they go, Jack; mark them down well. There, see! they settle just the other side of that dead pine beyond the fence. I can go to within a yard of them. Now, load up, Jack; and do you know, one of the great arts in upland shooting is to mark your birds down? it requires great experience to do it correctly, but by degrees the eye becomes accustomed to note everything by range, and experience teaches one to calculate distance to a nicety. Did you watch those dogs how instantly they came to heel and charged as soon as we had shot? See how nervously they await permission to gather the dead! And here let me say to you and impress upon you the necessity of never relaxing discipline in this respect; *always* load before sending your dog to *retrieve*. And another thing I want to tell you—never, under any circumstances, allow your dog to flush a bird; always flush him yourself. I have seen young sportsmen when a dog was pointing across a ditch, hie him on to get the bird up; never you do it, unless you want to irretrievably ruin your dog.   *   *   *

Now then, fetch dead bird, good dogs! Can't they understand English? Don't tell me! See them bring them in by the wing, without rumpling a feather. Catch them mouthing their birds! Isn't that perfection of instinct.

Come along now, I want to show you now that I marked those birds down correctly. I followed their flight with my eye, and saw that it was just in line with that pine stump, and as they darted down, I caught a glance at them just as they settled between yon clump of hazel bushes and yon stone fence. Come along quickly and we will walk around them and get between them and that piece of thickset swamp, otherwise they'll run in there and it will be a job to get them out, if we head them we would keep them in the open and get every mother's son of them. Now then, hie on, good dogs, so, steady. See how they watch me! Look at old "Shot," how intelligently he looks—Ha! they've got the scent. Steady, good dogs—to-ho! to-ho! to-ho!—wh-r, wh-r—bang, bang, bang, bang. Mark, John, mark! See, there they go down in that depression; they didn't fly far, did they. Are you loaded?—all right. Fetch dead birds, good dogs. There's one more. Seek dead, "Sport!" He's got him, sure enough. Well, that's three more;

and Jack, you fired behind those birds, and across my face in the bargain. You must never do that, it's a most unsportsman-like thing. When shooting always take the birds that rise on *your* side and leave the others for your companion ; and another thing, never get in advance of your companion, but walk in a line with him, otherwise you run the risk of his shooting you, and this is especially the case when hunting in thick underbrush, when you cannot always see each other; and when not within sight, you ought by constant signals, to be always aware of your companion's relative position.

None but a sportsman can understand the enthusiastic delight with which the gunner, after scattering a bevy, marks down and bags bird after bird, until every bird has been killed, nor the skill required in marking down single birds, and so handling the dogs as to inevitably lead them to the spot, and after having put them on the scent to keep them down to it till they find, nor the coolness necessarily exerted if the bird gets up under your feet, or just behind you as it often does.

Snap shooting is often practised in hunting quail, as they, when hard pressed, often take to thickets so dense that when they get up, you simply hear their whir-r-r, barely catching a glance at them. The November quail is a tough bird and strong of flight and requires a quick eye and a sharp shooting gun.

WOODCOCK.

Boys, the *agravatingest* bird that flies is the woodcock. His comings, his goings, his local habitation can not be calculated upon by any known rule; like the "little joker," you put your eye on him and he ain't there.

I am at present in a frame of mind peculiarly fit to enlarge upon this subject; indeed, if I had a tenpenny nail handy, I think I could give it the traditionary bite, for here it is the 4th of July, and by a happy train of circumstances the financial associations of New York have sagely decreed that there shall be two holidays this year instead of one. By this very sensible arrangement I have been able to compromise with you, giving *you* one day for fishing, and dedicating the other to the shooting of woodcock—so far so good; but now comes the provoking part of it: three weeks ago the whole country about

here was alive with birds; you couldn't walk
along the borders of a swamp but half a dozen
would flap up under your nose; you couldn't go
to a spring for a drink but one would cross your
line of vision; now there is not one to be seen.
Sportsmen are disgusted, having traveled miles
yesterday and never got a feather, the fact of the
matter being that the recent rains have flooded
the swamps and the birds are scattered all over
creation, so I must e'en stay at home. 'Tis an
ill wind, however, that blows no one any good,
and the unfortunate birds will have a little re-
spite, gain strength of wing, and perhaps hatch
another brood.

Of all the outrageously stupid laws ever enacted
that decree that woodcock may be shot after
the 1st of July is the most absurd, and why it
has not been rescinded through the influence of
sporting clubs I can not conceive. One might
with as much propriety shoot at a quail at this
season as at a woodcock. There is one conso-
lation, however, which is that a man who shoots
woodcock in July pays dear for his whistle, for
at that time birds secret themselves during the
day in the most impenetrable thickets and
marshes, where the atmosphere is made up of a
solution of sand-fly and hydrogen, of mosquito

and nitrogen, where the cat-briers interlace themselves and stretch themselves like cobwebs from twig to twig, and where no air can penetrate; here with a temperature of 100° Fahrenheit the sportsman lunges and plunges each step he makes, penetrating a foot or two in black mud, or catching in a net work of brambles, over which he stumbles head over heels, a friendly drapery of ivy armed with prickles as sharp as cambric needles catching him under the throat, while a white oak thorn penetrates the seat of his corduroy breeches. Meanwhile his dog is standing stiff as a poker on a bird in the midst of a morass so treacherous that he is afraid to attempt it. This is about the style of things in July, and ten to one if he does make a bag his birds spoil before he gets home.

Now, on the contrary, if these birds were left until October they would be fully grown, their numbers increased considerably, and they would then seek the upland, and the labors of the sportsman would be turned into pleasure.

But we must take things as we find them and pitch into the swamp like others. "Where are they to be found?" Why, everywhere from Canada to Louisiana, wherever you see a little streamlet trickling through rich black soil, there

5

you will find woodcock, along all our river bottoms, and frequently in dry seasons far out on
the meadows in the same localities with the
English snipe. You won't find many on Long
Island or in East Jersey, as they don't like a
sandy soil. Although shot at so constantly in
and out of season, they do not diminish materially in numbers from year to year. They make
appearance in this part of the country early in
the spring in their yearly emigration from the
south. They begin laying in May, and it is asserted hatch two broods, if not three. They lay
four or five eggs each time, and they very
rapidly arrive at maturity. They moult in July
and frequently disappear most unaccountably
for weeks, returning quite as mysteriously.
Their flight, like the snipe's, is apt to take place
on a moonlight night. The woodcock is always
in this part of the world hunted with a setter
dog, as no pointer could with his short hair and
thin skin, not to speak of his aversion to water,
penetrate the thickets and morasses; and even
the setter, brave as he is, sometimes refuses to
go in, and oftentimes comes out covered with
blood or overcome by the heat. The sportsman
to hunt woodcock successfully should have his
dog completely under control and should never

let him range out of sight if he can avoid it, otherwise he may miss him altogether and leave him standing on a bird. The mode of shooting woodcock is peculiar. Oftentimes you barely catch a glimpse of the bird as he flits past you in the thicket, and you fire, without the possibility of accurate aim, in the *direction* of his flight. This is called snap shooting and is done so quickly that the gun oftentimes doesn't touch the shoulder. Of course there is a good deal of chance about this, although men who do a great deal of this kind of shooting, frequently by intuition seemingly, manage to kill a great many birds. Of course one wants a light and short gun, the usual charge being 2½ drams powder to an ounce of No. 10 shot. The shooting rig for this sort of work should be a suit of the heaviest linen drill, a light wide-awake hat, a pair of old hole-y light boots, and a pair of old buckskin gloves; the last being indispensable to save the hands being torn.

THE DOG.

Boys, did you ever see a city man, who had never ridden behind anything but an omnibus horse all his life, come into the country with a wide-awake hat, a bird's-eye cravat and horse-shoe pin, and a cut-away coat? Did you ever see such an individual critically examine a horse, take him by the nose and look at his teeth, pass his hand over his withers and down his legs, and then oracularly give *his opinion* of the animal, in the language, *verbatim*, as contained in a "horse" article in the last week's *Spirit?*

Well, so it is, boys, often with amateur sportsmen in their judgment of the canine race. A biped (looking very much like an animated toothpick) swaggers up to you, chirps to your dog (who, taking him in at a glance, gives a premonitory growl and subsides with his head between his fore-paws), and delivers himself in this wise: "Irish setter, isn't he?" (the dog is an English pointer); "looks very much like a strain we had with us in the Peninsula; they were a little beefy, to be sure, at first, but army fare and hard work, when we were not under fire, soon got them into condition." This is about the style of thing that very young gentlemen get off about hunting dogs, of which they know about as much as a cow does of a ruffled shirt; indeed, many people who do shoot, and shoot well too, talk a monstrous deal of nonsense in this regard. It's not an uncommon thing to hear comments like this : " Fine-looking setter, that of yours! Should judge him to be Irish. Got a fine double nose, too; nothing like double nose for scent!" Now, this is, of course, the purest and most absolute "*rot*," for, so far as I can discover, the Irish setter never has a double nose, it being in reality not a double nose at all, but a *deformity*, like the hair-lip in human beings, and a peculiarity of the French breed. Indeed, Youatt asserts that it not only is not an advantage, but that it positively interferes with the acuteness of the scent.

This ignorance on the part of sportsmen renders them peculiarly liable to be cheated by dog dealers. In our district, within a circuit of five miles say, there are perhaps a hundred so-called hunting dogs, and it is probable that they are held at an average price of $50 each, some being held as high as $250. Now, it is safe to assert that at least two-thirds of these dogs are "curs,"

not worth the powder to blow them up with! It
is true they may be made to stand on a bird, and
perhaps retrieve it, but they are in no way to be
depended upon, and after an hour's hunting
would be worse than useless; in fact, any dog
may be taught that. You may laugh, but I can
cite a case in point.

Some years ago, Mr. S.—whom you know, and
who used to shoot a good deal with Judge N.—
one day, taking a holiday, went out into the fields
with his gun and a dog which he had imported,
to ask the Judge to go with him and try to pick
up a few quail, and see how the new dog worked.
The Squire, nothing loathe, started off, and after
proceeding a short distance found that a favorite
terrier had stealthily followed him: In vain he
endeavored to drive him back, and at last gave it
up, much, however, to Mr. S.'s annoyance, who
remonstrated with him on the impropriety of so
doing. The Squire, who had looked over Mr.
S.'s dog, and only from deference to his owner
had refrained from pronouncing him a cur, being
a little irritated, offered to lay a wager that his
terrier would point as many birds as Mr. S.'s
imported setter. The wager was taken. The
shooting ground was in the open on the edge of
a meadow, and the dogs were both thrown off

The terrier set to work artistically, found the first bird, and stood as stiff as a stake and retrieved him when shot, and pointed and retrieved five birds successively, while the setter found but two. The terrier was a remarkably sharp little customer, had often accompanied the Squire to the fields in his farming operations, with his friend the setter (a famous dog of the Squire's), and had got the hang of the thing, which peculiarity the Squire, on becoming aware of, had succeeded for his amusement in developing.

Pigs even are gifted with a remarkably acute scent—indeed, necessarily so to enable them to perceive their food (when in a wild state) to a considerable depth under the surface. Some years ago an English sportsman, discovering a sow in his possession to be endowed with unusual instinct, and being aware of the delicacy of scent in swine, conceived the idea of training the sow to point game, and after patient training succeeded, and the pig actually became fond of the sport, and showed manifestations of pleasure when her master appeared, gun in hand. This goes to show that a dog that will point his bird is not necessarily a hunting dog, any more than a parrot that is taught to talk is endowed with human understanding; and also that in nothing is there a greater field for fraud than in buying and selling hunting dogs. A business man, who only shoots a dozen times a year, in buying a dog and witnessing his performances, if he finds and retrieves his bird, is pretty sure to pay the price asked without further trial, although he may be absolutely worthless.

The only advice that I could volunteer to a young sportsman in the purchase of a dog, would be to buy him of, or through, some sportsman of note, who is thoroughly acquainted with the strain or lineage of the dog, for blood will tell in a dog as well as in a horse, and if a pup is " sired" and " grandsired" by good stock, he is a safe purchase. It's no use taking a pup to a " dog breaker" and asking *his advice*, for they don't enjoy the reputation of saints, and it's ten to one they tell you that there is no doubt of the purity of the pup's breed, etc., etc., and advise his being put in training. I remember an instance of this kind which occurred here not long since. A friend of ours was presented with a " pup." He took it to a breaker who was in ecstacies over him, and it was at once decided to put him in training; three months afterwards the trainer announced his education complete, and on an appointed day brought " Bang," and a

DOG OF HIS OWN to show his performance in the field. I was invited to assist. We got in among two or three bevies of quail; the trainer's own dog found, pointed and retrieved beautifully; the new graduate watched his canine mentor and *lay down on his back and kicked*, on every occasion that the old dog pointed. The trainer explained it as a *peculiarity* of a certain strain of dog, but he couldn't make him retrieve, even in a *peculiar* way, and finally bullied our friend out of $75, training fee! The dog never had been and never was good for anything. The trainer had simply held him with a check string when in the field and whenever the old dog pointed, he pounded "Bang," until he *crouched too*, the result being that so soon as a companion found his bird, he, in sheer fright, lay on his back and appealed for mercy.

My advice to you boys is, if any one ever makes you a present of a pup, train him yourself. The only art is kindness, indeed the exercise of the Christian virtues of patience, forbearance and perseverance. If a dog is thoroughbred, it is the easiest and pleasantest task imaginable, indeed some dogs actually require no training; so far as finding and pointing go, but these are the *great exceptions.* Now we will suppose some

5*

friend of the family, entirely reliable, sends you
a pup; he has got over his babyhood, distemper,
etc., and is at an age when he should be sent to
school. You take him out on the lawn, tie a
light cord to his collar and let him play about,
suddenly you say, loudly and decidedly, *charge!*
checking him at the same time with the cord,
and walking up, put your hand on his back and
press him down; he resists, but you are firm,
speaking gently and shaking your finger at him.
Soon he discovers what you want and that he
isn't going to be hurt, and lies quiet; in a minute
or two he wants to resume his gambol, you again
press him forcibly down, speaking harshly, and
so on for half an hour; you then caress and feed
him. The next day, and the next, you give him
a lesson and in a week he will *charge.* The next
thing to teach him is to charge at a distance;
the check string is again resorted to, as long a
one as the grounds will admit; having been kept
up a day or two, he will naturally rush off;
before he gets to the end of his rope you shout
charge and check him severely; he will instinctively *come to charge* from the effects of previous
lessons, but seeing you at a distance he, yearning
for his gallop, will, ten to one, try to get off
again; here great patience must be shown, but

firmness of purpose and threatening gestures
must be put into practice, with an admonitory
cut of the dog whip, and this lesson must be
continued day after day, and after each lesson
the dog caressed and fed. Dogs, like some boys
I know, often get ugly and sullen, and to whip
them only makes them worse, therefore kindness
is by far the best treatment in every case, as no
nature can resist it in the end. Supposing after
several weeks you have succeeded in teaching
your dog to charge under every circumstance,
now, then, it is important that he should be
taught the absolute necessity of "*coming in to
heel,*" when ordered so to do in obedience to the
word *close,* and such obedience can be taught by
pursuing the foregoing system. He may now be
taught to retrieve ; and a good plan I have found
to practice is to let him get very hungry, then,
attaching a bone to a cord, to drag it over the
grass, and finally hiding it in a clump of bushes.
The dog is then let out, and the check cord attached; he, of course, snuffing about, soon strikes
scent of the beef, and in a moment has it in his
mouth. You then call out sharply "fetch;" he
looks, but don't understand. You then haul him
in, and taking the bone away from him, again
hide it, he seeking and again finding it, again

being ordered to *fetch* and again hauled in. Here the utmost patience is needed, but before the lesson is over he will probably of his own accord fetch the bone, which he then must be allowed to gnaw, and he must likewise be caressed. He will soon get the hang of this, especially if his hunger is only appeased after obedience. All this will take weeks to accomplish. He must now be taught to *give up* what he *fetches*—no easy task, but patience will conquer. Being thoroughly broken to *fetch* a piece of beef or a bird, he must be taught not to *mouth* or tear it. This is taught by some in this wise : A ball of rags, through which half-a-dozen nails are driven so that the blunted ends obtrude say a quarter of an inch, is saturated with beef drippings, and is hidden in the grass, and the dog told to *fetch*. He grabs the ball as ravenously as the bone, when, of course, the nails stick in him, and he drops it like a hot potato ; but *fetch* he must, and finally does, holding it as gingerly as possible. A few dozen repetitions of this, and he will never mouth a bird or anything else. His home education complete, he is taken into the field, held in check by the cord. If he is a good dog and there are birds about, he will strike the scent and finally bring up on a point. Now is a critical time; you should approach steadily, and as you get up to him, if he shows the slightest disposition to run in on the birds, he must be checked violently, and if he again attempts it a few cuts with a dog whip should be given. If you put the bird up and shoot it, the command *charge* and *close* must be given simultaneously and *enforced strictly*. You then load up, and utter sharply *fetch dead bird*. It is best, of course, to be accompanied during the first lessons in the field with a steady, well-trained dog and a companion to manage check rope or to shoot. A few lessons in the field will thoroughly develop the dog, and he then must be taught to *hunt*, quarter the field, etc., meanwhile obedient to your every gesture and paying strict attention to the premonitory whistle.

Boys, you once saw Rarey! you saw how he fairly enslaved the savage "Cruiser" by patience and kindness. So you, by exercise of those virtues, can lead and teach a good dog as well and better than any professional breaker.

The majority of hunting dogs in this country are setters. Their docility, their fondness for water, their natural aptitude for retrieving, their long and thick coating of hair, which serves as an armor against briars and thorns, make them

far preferable to pointers, who, although pos-
sessed of keen scent and peculiarly fitted for
hunting over open stubble fields, are comparatively useless from their dread of water, and
their thin delicate coats in the thick under-
growth where we shoot most of our game. It
seems almost an absurdity to offer the foregoing
suggestions as to dog training in such a very
general way as I have done, but any very ex-
tended or explicit directions would be out of
place here, and I can only refer you to very ex-
haustive treatises by Herbert, Youatt, Hutchin-
son and others.

BOAT SAILING.

BOATING.

A knowledge of boating is as essential almost to a sportsman as the ability to use his gun, for, as a general thing, in fowl-shooting the gunner reaches his shooting ground across wide bays and lakes, and in fishing, a boat is nearly always an indispensable adjunct to his sport. American boys, as a general thing, can handle an oar or wield a paddle, but very few, comparatively, understand the management of the sailing boat. Hence, I will assume that *you* know nothing whatever about it, and will commence by quoting that trite saying, "A little knowledge is a dangerous thing," which is in no case better exemplified than in one's ignorantly attempting to handle a boat under sail, for nothing but experience can teach one how to do it.

It's a difficult matter to attempt even to familiarize a boy with the technicalities of boat sailing; but, nevertheless, it strikes me that in order to convey a clear conception of the mode of propelling a boat by sails, the attempt should be made to give an explanation of the various terms used in so doing, and I will endeavor to do it by narrating in detail some of my own early experiences in boat sailing. I well remember that when I first undertook to sail a boat—which, by the way, was a small bateau that I had rigged with an old table-cloth for a sail, my model being taken from a picture in an old magazine— I was completely nonplussed and disgusted to find that I could not make the boat go *directly* toward any particular spot, if the wind were blowing *from that direction,* for at that time my ideas of a *head wind* were exceedingly misty. As soon as my sail was hoisted, my bateau would insist upon going off in *another* direction from the one which I desired to go, but slid off with the wind, or before what I did not then know was a *fair wind.* This was bad enough, but when I wanted to stop her, not then knowing enough to bring her head round in the direction of the wind, or in nautical parlance to LUFF her up and then stop her way, I went bang at the river's bank, when both captain and mast went overboard together. Thus ended my first day's sailing, for I had to lay her up for repairs. Nothing deterred, however, by my ducking, shipwreck or parental injunction, but enriched with the previous day's experience, I again got under way, bearing in mind, however, that just before the collision referred to, as I was nearing the bank, a gruff voice had sung out "luff, you beggar you, luff," so I at once came to the proper appreciation of the euphonious word, and several times repeated the nautical manœuvre of *coming to* with great success. Thus far, therefore, I had learned practically what was a *fair wind*, what was a *head wind*, and how to *stop* a boat, and the meaning and proper application of the word *luff*. * * * At about one mile's distance from my anchorage, precisely in the direction from which the wind blew, or *dead to windward*, a field sloped down to the water's edge, and that field was planted with peach trees, and those peach trees were loaded with luscious fruit. The road of this orchard was closely guarded, but the river-front was unfortified, and I knew it, and I wanted some of those peaches, but how to get there in my bateau I couldn't for the life of me tell; for I found that when I turned the boat's head in that direction, that the wind, blowing directly in front of the sail, almost flapped the mast out of her, but would not fill it. That would never do, so I turned her head a little to one side, when, of course, the sail filled at once and the clipper moved off. Instinctively I hauled in the rope fastened to the end of the sail, and headed the boat as near the point of the orchard as she would go without her sails flapping, and I found that the more I hauled the rope, the nearer she would head up for the point; but after going on thus for some time, I found that she must soon strike the bank, and without at all intending it, but while trying to make her keep heading up, the sail suddenly gave a flap and the boat a turn, the sail filling on the *other side*. Finding that, although partially turned around, she still tended up the river, or toward the point, I let her go on, and on arriving at and trying to edge up the opposite bank, the sail flapped again and around went the boat, and she again filled on the other side; and now to my gratification I saw that I was gaining ground, and became convinced that if I repeated these manœuvres I should eventually gain my destination. I did not, however, then know that this manœuvre was nautically styled *"beating to windward,"* and that each time the boat went round that she was *tacking*.

My patience and forbearance were finally rewarded, and I gained the orchard, when, having filled my pockets and stomach with peaches, I had just shoved off again when I was discovered, and an irate man and a villainous-looking dog rushed to the river bank. This time I had a fair wind, but I did not know enough to pay out the sail rope or sheet, but kept it as before, close hauled in, when beating up; consequently my progress was slow, and I was still within reach of stones and peaches with which the enraged individual aforesaid was keeping up a lively fusilade. At this juncture a rotten peach, better aimed than the others, took me alongside of the head. Didn't I jump? and in so doing some six feet of the sheet ran through my hand, when simultaneously the boat gave a bound, and in a moment I was out of reach, and had learned by new experience that in going before the wind you must *ease off the sheet.*

Rejoicing in my success as a navigator, munching my peaches and lazily holding the sheet, on approaching a bend in the river I slightly altered the course in order to get by the point, when all of a sudden I found myself in the river, my peaches afloat and my bateau bottom upward! Half an hour after, however, found the yacht all right, and me drying myself on the meadow, soliloquizing as to the cause of the accident.

On thinking the matter over, I remembered

that the sail was full, and that it was over the right side of the boat, and that just as I altered her direction to round the point, the wind, which had been directly behind me, or *astern*, blew suddenly on the right side of my face, and that in a second the sail was forced violently over to the other side of the boat, the jerk capsizing her ; in fact, I had involuntarily performed the manœuvre of JIBING, and my cogitations led me to the conclusion that if, when I found it necessary to alter her course and thus bring the wind a little more on the side, I had hauled in the sheet quickly and allowed the sail to shift over to the other side gradually, no accident would have occurred.

Thus in two days I had become practically acquainted with some vital principles in the art of boat sailing.

I was, at the time referred to, spending some time in the house of an uncle, a retired naval officer, genus sea-dog, who religiously preserved the relics of by-gone days, and consequently I was never at a loss for small ropes or blocks wherewith to rig my bateau, and I soon became ambitious to have a boat rigged after the style of a very pretty schooner, a model of which graced my uncle's sanctum; and, after several weeks' hard work, I succeeded in getting her under jib, foresail and mainsail; and, better still, cajoled my uncle into being an accomplice, in so much as to give his advice and assistance unknown to my aunt, who would at once have tabooed the whole affair. The old gentleman, horrified at my ignorance of terms nautical, would sit for hours on the river's bank (at a safe distance from the house), and puffing his cigar, would deliver himself in this wise: "Now, you young monkey, don't you forget that the rope attached to the outer end or clew of the sail is called a *sheet;* now, for instance, that rope which hauls the jib aft is the *jibsheet*, and those attached to the clews of the foresail and mainsail are called respectively the *foresheet* and *mainsheet* (lubbers are apt to call the sail itself the sheet). The spar to which the foot of your sail is fasteened is the BOOM, and the light spar to which the head is made fast is the GAFF. The sides of the sails are called the *leaches;* the lower and *outer* corner, the *clew;* the lower and *inner* corner, the *tack;* the bottom of the sail is called the *foot;* the top is called the *head;* the upper and *inner* corner, the *throat;* the upper and *outer* corner is the *peak*—(the term *throat*, though thus applied, properly designates the jaws of the GAFF."

"The halliards, as you know, are the ropes by

which the sail is hoisted—the throat halliards, of course, hoisting the inner part of the sail, while the peak halliards hoist the outer end of the gaff. The rope which is permanent or *standing*, and leads from the top of the foremast to the end of the bowsprit, is the *forestay* or *jibstay*, and the ropes which lead from the mast-head down on either side, and are fastened to the side of the boat, are called *backstays;* and the rope leading from the mast-head to the end of the boom (to support it) is called the *topping-lift*."

All this, and oceans more of the same sort, the old gentleman imparted to me in accents tinged with sympathetic pity, evidently saddened at the conviction that a boy, and that boy his nephew, should have reached the mature age of ten years in such gross and benighted ignorance, which clearly proved the degeneracy of the age.

As my nautical proclivities developed, I was informed that no one was qualified to handle a boat who could not furl a sail properly, or, in case of a strong breeze, reef her down, and that it was likewise indispensable to be able to tie a square knot and to splice a rope; and warming up with the subject, the old gentleman despatched me to his sanctum, intrusting me with the key of a mysterious chest with rope handles, which was

popularly supposed by the family to contain
Spanish dollars and jewels of untold value, cap-
tured from pirates on the Spanish main; hence,
the custody of this key was a mark of prime
favoritism, and was accompanied by the injunction to "bear a hand, you lubberly young rascal,
and fetch me a canvass bag you'll find in the
port side, and mind don't you touch anything
else." Of course I went off feeling very big and
important, and returned bearing a great dirty
canvass bag as tenderly as if it had been a new-
born babe. The bag on being opened emitted,
I must say, a very nasty smell, rancid tallow and
tar being the prominent scents; however, I soon
became used to that. I brought out successively
the following articles: Balls of spun yarn, sail
twine, needles, palms, marling-spike, tin boxes
with mixture of tar and grease, pieces of canvass,
Manilla rope, marling-spikes and fids, which,
being duly spread out, I was initiated into their
names and uses; and the hours passed in the
acquirement of those early lessons in seamanship
are among my pleasantest recollections; and so
necessary is it for boys handling boats to understand how to tie a few of the simpler knots and
put two ends of a rope together, that I have
caused to be inserted here the subjoined plate,

with accompanying instructions, which will doubt-
less prove plain enough for you to follow and perfect yourself therein.

It would be inappropriate if not impossible to
attempt within the contracted limits of this article to teach you how to make all the various
splices, knots, etc., required in rigging and working a boat, but the plate on the opposite page,
and the accompanying directions referring thereto, are well worth your study, as by it you will
be enabled by the aid of a piece of Manilla rope
and a marling-spike to master the art of putting
two ends of a rope together, of making an eye-
splice and three *knots*, a knowledge of which
would always be useful to you whether in or out
of a boat.

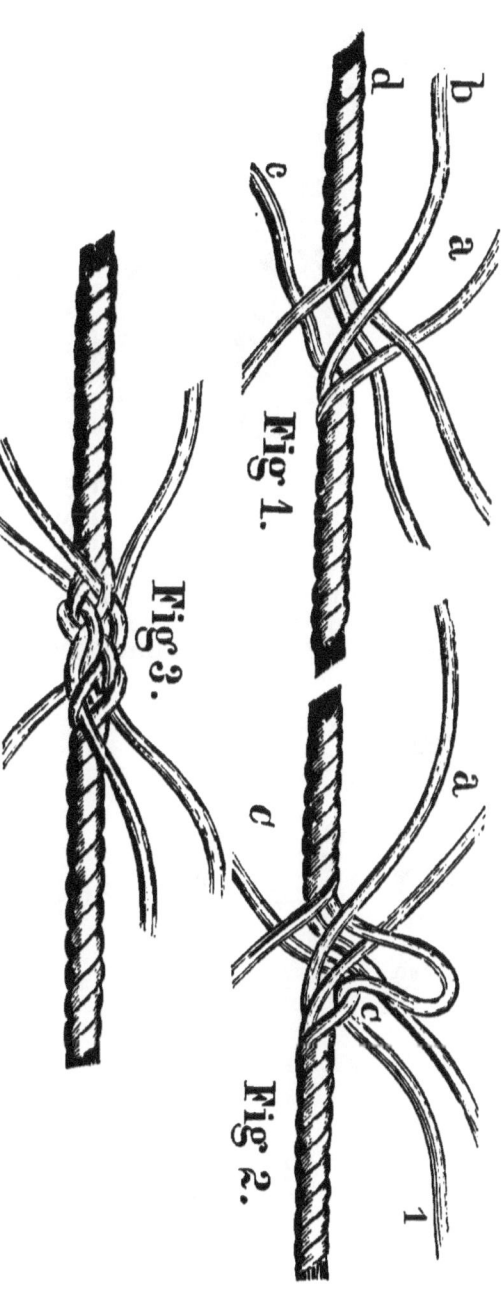

Fig. 1.

Fig. 2.

Fig. 3.

A SHORT SPLICE.

To splice the two ends of a rope *together*, proceed thus: Unlay the strands for a convenient length ; then take an end in each hand, place them one within the other (Fig. 1), and draw them close. Hold the strands (*a*, *b*. *c*) and the end of the rope (*d*) fast in the left hand, or, if the rope be large, stop them down with a rope yarn ; then take the middle end (1), pass it over the strand (*a*), and, having opened it with the thumb, or a marling spike, (Fig. 2), push it through under the strand (*c*) and haul it taut. Perform the same operation with the other ends, by leading them *over* the first next to them, and *through* under the second, on both sides ; the splice will then appear like Fig. 3 ; but in order to render it more secure the work must be repeated, leading the ends *over* the third and *through* the fourth ; or the ends may be untwisted, scraped down with a knife, tapered, marled and served over with spun-yarn.

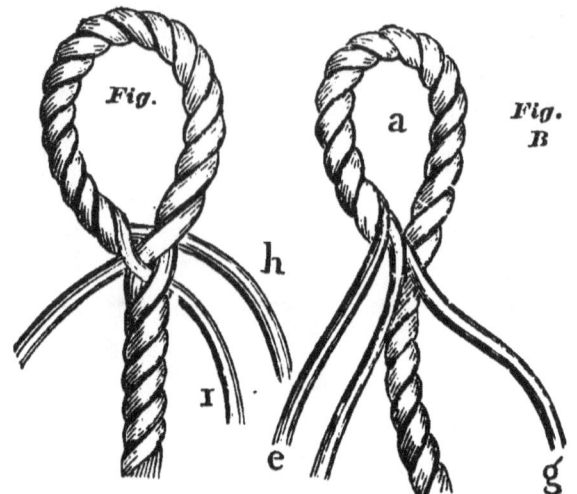

AN EYE SPLICE, Fig. A.

Is made by opening the end of a rope and laying the strands (*e, f, g*) at any distance upon the standing part, forming the collar or eye (*a*). The end (*h*), Fig. B, is pushed through the strand next to it (having previously opened it with a marling-spike); the end (*i*) is taken *over* the same strand and through the second; and the end (*k*) through the third, on the other side.

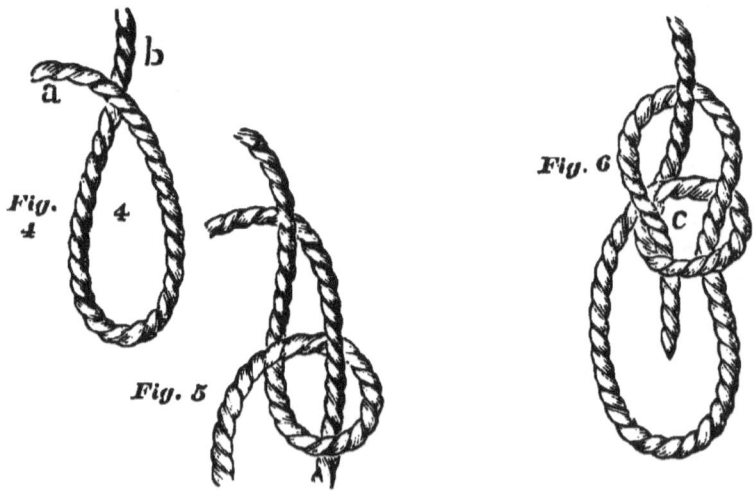

TO MAKE A BOW-LINE KNOT, Fig. 6.

Take the end of a rope (*a*), Fig. 4, in the right hand, and the standing part (*b*) in the left, laying the end over the standing part; with the left hand turn a bight of the *standing* part over it, Fig. 5; lead the end round the standing part through the bight again and it will appear like Fig. 6.

Fig. 7

TO MAKE A RUNNING BOW-LINE KNOT, Fig. 7.

Take the end of a rope, Fig. 6, round the standing yart (*b*) and through the bight (*c*): make the single bow-line knot upon the part (*d*), and it is done, Fig. 7.

Fig. 8

HITCHING A ROPE, Fig. 8.

Is performed thus:—Pass the end of a rope (*b*) round the standing part; bring it up through the bight, and seize it to the standing part at (*d*). This is called a *Half-hitch*. Two of these one above the other, Fig. 8, called a *Clove-hitch*.

Fig. 9

TO MAKE AN OVER-HAND KNOT, Fig. 9.

Pass the end of a rope (*a*) over the standing part (*b*) and through the bight above (*c*).

Fig. 10

Fig. 11

TO MAKE A REEF-KNOT, OR SQUARE KNOT.

Make an over-hand knot as before directed, Fig. 10, round a yard or spar: bring the end (*a*) (being the next towards you) over to the *left*, and (*b*) to the right, take (*a*) round (*b*), draw them taut, and it is done, Fig. 11. If the ends are crossed the wrong way it is called a *Granny-knot*.

"Now, boy, as you can put two ends of a rope together, and have left off making granny knots, and have fitted your sail with reef points, I'll give you a lesson in reefing. Jump into your boat and stand off twenty or thirty yards." No sooner said than done; and the commodore waddling down to the bank, and making a trumpet of his hand, sings out in a voice only equal to that of Barnum's lion, which had passed through our place a few days previously, "Luff her up close to wind, so! don't let her come about, you jackanapes! so! that's right. Now, then, ease off your jibsheet, haul your foresail to windward, so! Now, then, haul in your mainsheet, so! belay that! Now, you see, SHE'S HOVE TO; don't forget that."

REEFING.

"Now, then, lower away your peak halliards, so! belay that! Lower away on your throat until the sail settles down as far as the single reef points, so! that'll do! belay that! Now, then, cast off your tack. Take that piece of Manilla rope and make one end fast to the cringle on the after leach of the sail, opposite to the single reef points, taking the other end through the cringle by which the after part of the sail is made fast to the boom, and bring it back through the cringle where it was first made fast. Now, then, haul taut and bring the end of the rope down under and up around the boom and through the cringle, again repeating this twice, and then hitch it around its own standing part. Now, then, tie up your single reef points, beginning at the outer ends, bringing them around the foot of the sail and not around the boom; and mind you make square knots, you monkey you! There, that's right! Now take that other small piece of rope, and pass it through the inner cringle next the mast, opposite the single reef points, and then through the lower cringle, where it's made fast to the jaws of the boom, and hauling taut, make fast to its standing part. Now you have taken in your single reef, you can hoist your sail. If you want to double-reef your sail, it is better always to take in a single reef first, so that, if the wind moderates, you can turn out one reef at a time."

"You are now under single-reefed mainsail. Now, then, I'll teach you how to furl your sail. Lower away your mainsail gradually, and gather it in so as not to wet it; get your gaff snug down on your boom ; haul the slack of your sail over the boom and lay the after leach over the slack, hauling taut from the end of the gaff; and now, then, roll your loose sail snug up to the gaff, but don't roll it around the boom or gaff. Now, then, pass your lashings. There, that'll do, boy; come ashore and make your boat fast. Now, don't you forget it ever, the port or larboard side is the *left* side, and the starboard is the *right* side of a boat; so when I order you to put your helm hard-a-port, shove the tiller over as far as it will go to the port side, when, if you will look over the stern, you will find that the broad part of the rudder is over on the starboard, and as the vessel goes through the water, the water running past it, it meets this obstacle and pushes the stern over to *port*, but the bow to *starboard;* hence the order *hard-a-port* is given when you want your boat turned to starboard, or the right hand side, and the order *hard-a-starboard* is given when you want your boat turned to port, or to the left hand side. Sometimes it so happens that you are in a narrow channel where the tide or current runs swiftly, and you want to drop your boat downstream without turning, or stern first, so remember that in going astern you must turn your helm in the *same* direction that you want your boat's head turned. The terms hard-a-port and hard-a-starboard are not used in sailing vessels, excepting in going dead before the wind. When a vessel has the wind ahead, abeam or quartering, if it is desirable to bring her closer to the wind, the order is given to *luff*, or if she is to be turned more away from the direction of the wind, the order is given to *keep away*. If you want to "tack," you order the tiller put *hard down*, or hard-a-lee, which means as far over on the side away from the wind as possible, which will, of course, force her head into the wind; but if you want to turn her away from the wind as far as possible, you order the tiller put *hard up*.

When a vessel is beating to windward, she is said to be on the starboard-tack if the wind blows on her *starboard side*, and on the port-tack if the wind blows on the *port side*.

A boat having a fair wind must give way to a vessel on the wind or beating, or, as it is termed, *close-hauled*, and boats close-hauled on the starboard-tack keep on their course, while vessels on the **port**-tack must give way."

TRIMMING SAILS.

Nothing but experience, as I have often told you, can teach a boy how to trim his sails, but a hint may assist him in giving him an idea how it should be done—why certain sails should be

hauled aft at one time, and at others given all
the sheet they can take. On looking back a
page or two, you will observe that when I began
to sail a boat I discovered by accident that
when I wanted to reach a place that lay in the
direction from whence the wind came, I had to
haul in my sheets flat, thus bringing the wind
on my *weather* bow, and I found that unless the
sails had been flattened in, the wind could not
have got any hold upon them ; but I also discovered that every foot that the wind veered in
the direction of the stern of the boat, the greater
the hold did it take upon the sails and the more
the sheets could be eased off. For instance, the
wind is North and your boat is heading up nearly
Northeast ; this makes a very small angle for
the wind to act ; in a little while, however, the
wind hauls NNW, which brings it more on the
side, and you ease off your sheet. Soon it gets
round to West, which brings it abeam, and you
ease off still more and finally it goes round SW
and you let your sheet run entirely out, the wind
being dead astern.

Thus we see that as we edge off from the wind,
or the wind hauls in our favor as the case may
be, we gradually pay out sheet, and as we edge
up *toward the wind*, or it hauls ahead, we haul or

6*

flatten in the sheets. *Full and By* is the nautical term applied to the act of beating to windward ; as, although you must keep your boat *by* the wind, or as near as possible to it, still you must, in order to make any headway, keep her sails *full.* To sail near the wind as possible, keeping your sails full at the same time, is a very nice operation in boat sailing, and can only be done by strict watchfulness and attention. Oftentimes a boat, though duller than her competitor, wins a race through the carefulness in this respect of the person steering ; for instance, you are sailing in a regatta, your course lays past a certain point, faster boats than yours have tried to *weather* it or get past it without making a tack, but have failed and been obliged to make a short tack off shore. You think *you* can manage it and thus snatch the prize from the faster boats ; you edge your boat along, the leach of your sail just quivering, but your sail full ; when you get nearly abreast of the point, you give her a good full and then suddenly shove her up into the wind, and by the impetus thus gained she runs a considerable distance right in the wind's eye ; not letting her lose her headway however, you then fill away on her again, and under renewed impulse you again luff her up into the wind, and successfully repeating the manœuvre several times, you find yourself *by* the point without the necessity of making a tack, and consequently to windward and far in advance of your competitors.

Putting a boat about on another tack, **or** *going in stays*, as it is termed, is a very nice operation, and if done bunglingly occasions great loss of time, as the boat is of course drifting to leeward all the time after she loses her way, and as in failing to go around, or missing stays, as it is called, the boat is for the time being uncontrolable, if in a sea-way her position is perilous, as she may capsize or have a sea break aboard of her.

TACKING.

Let us suppose we are beating down a bay and have stood as far over on one tack as is expedient and have to *go about.* The first thing to be done is to see that the jib-sheet is all clear and ready to let go. We then give her a good full, after which the tiller is turned gradually to leeward, bringing the boat up into the wind, and as soon as the after-leach of the main-sail begins to shake, the helm is put hard down, and the sails are shaking in the wind ; she has still way on her though, and the great thing is not to let her lose her momentum; the jib-sheet is then let fly, and if she hangs and does'nt look like going round, the jib is hauled over to windward to help swing her, while the tiller, which was hard down, is now put amidships so as not to be a drag on her; as soon as her head begins to pay off and the jib begins to fill, the jib-sheet is haul'd flat aft, and the main-boom is swung over, and the tiller put down a bit to meet her and bring her up, "*full and by*" again.

In steering a boat the tiller should never be shoved violently up and down like a pump handle, as it interferes materially with the speed of the boat, yawing her all over creation; if a boat be properly ballasted she requires very little movement of the tiller, and the proper ballasting and trim of a sailing boat is vitally important. If she is too much loaded forward or *by the head* she would have a tendency to be running up into the wind, which is termed carrying a *weather helm*; if, on the contrary, she should be down by the stern, she will have a tendency to turn away from the wind, which is called carrying a *lee helm*. Indeed, a boat to sail well, should be on an even keel, neither by the head or stern. A convenient ballast for a large boat is fresh water in very small breakers, or little barrels, holding from 5 to 10 gallons, which carry the advantage of being so bouyant that should the boat capsize, the water casks will buoy her up, whereas stone or sand ballast would carry her down.

The art of bringing a boat to her anchorage or to her wharf is a very important thing to learn and should be practised frequently, and may, under certain circumstances, be done under full sail with impunity, provided it is properly done. If the desired point to bring up is dead to windward, keep a good full on her until you think she has momentum enough to fetch, then haul down your jib and shove her up into the wind; if the anchorage be to leeward, let her go until she is abreast of her mooring, then luff her up into the wind and haul down her jib, when she will soon lose her headway and drift down on her anchorage or to the wharf. If obliged to run in before the wind and there is no room to luff her up into the wind, then, as she approaches, haul down your jib and lower away your mainsail until there is just enough left to carry her in.

It would be absurd for me here to attempt a disquisition upon boats or to recommend any particular style; according to my notion, however, a little cat-rigged boat, partly decked over, is the safest and handiest small sail-boat that floats, it being the easiest handled and most convenient ; the mast being stepped in her bow, or "right in the eyes of her," she has but one sail; this sail hoists by halliards, like any other, and the halliards, instead of being made fast to pins at the foot of the mast, are led through small blocks and brought aft and made fast to pins which are fixed in the after thwart or seat, just in front of the steersman, and he thus has complete control over her sail and can lower it at pleasure, should the weather be puffy, or he can, by throwing off the pin all but a single turn of the throat and peak halliards, and holding the slack in his hand, ease off either the one or the other at pleasure, so that in a second, in case of a sudden squall striking the boat, he can let everything go by the run. Where there is but one man to manage a boat, I should decidedly give the preference to the cat-rig. The handiest little boat for shooting, par excellence, that I know of, or for fishing either, is a boat used extensively in Barnegat Bay, called a sneak boat or box. It is built precisely in the form of an old-fashioned, round-toed shoe, decked over with the exception of a square hatch, just large enough

for a man to get inside of. This boat is about
ten feet long, flat-bottomed, square stern, and
draws, when loaded, about five or six inches
water ; the floor is flat from the stern about two-
thirds forward, and then it slopes upward at a
considerable angle, like the sole of a round-toed
shoe does, and thus one is enabled to shove its
bows over the low mud banks and hide it among
the sea-weed while the rest of the boat is afloat.
As the bottom slopes upward, the bow slopes
downward, making a perfect wedge. As the oc-
cupant sits on a little bench, an inch or two
above the bottom, just high enough to keep him
off the damp planks, he is below the center of
gravity, and consequently the little boat, under
sail, is as stiff as a church, and, being very often
built with a tiny little center-board, it is astonishing how they will work to windward. The mast
is not over five feet long, and the sail rigged
with a sprit, not much larger than a good sized
pocket handkerchief, but there being so little
resistance it is astonishing how they will bowl
along. Being very low forward, it is natural to
suppose that they would ship a great deal of
water, especially from the peculiar form of the
bow, which suggests a strong propensity to run
under a heavy sea ; to avoid this, a semi-circular

piece of heavy canvas is tacked down to the deck just forward of the hatch, and when it is rough a small stick, one end of which fits into an eye on its upper edge and the other end in a small indentation in the deck, stretches and holds this canvas in position, about 18 inches high, making a complete breakwater. The gunner arranges his decoy ducks and geese on the stern and bow of his little "box," and his gun in a little rack alongside him, and hoisting his miniature sail, bears away for his ducking point, perhaps miles away.   *   *   *   *

It is always convenient, no matter how small your boat, especially if she be a boat kept for shooting or fishing, to have a round hole cut through her forward thwart and a step in her keel, so that when you have the wind any way fair you can step a light mast and make sail on her—and a favorite and appropriate rig for this purpose is a *sprit sail*. This sail is generally very light, and laced to the mast, having no boom or gaff, but is stretched out by means of a pole called a sprit (or spreet), one end of which fits in a loop on the outer and upper corner of the sail and the other end in a loop about half-way down the mast; this pole crosses the sail diagonally. The sail is easily stowed, being wrapt with the sprit pole around the mast, lashed with the sheet and placed fore and aft in the boat, not interfering at all with the rowing; when, the wind coming fair, the mast is lifted up and placed through the hole into its step, the lashing cast off, the one end of the sprit shoved into the loop at the outer corner of the sail and the other end forced into the loop on the mast; the sheet is then made fast and she glides off, relieving the labor of rowing.

Here are some general rules which, in handling a sail-boat, should never be lost sight of, viz:

1st. Always have your sheets and halliards clear, and ready to let go; if they are nicely coiled away, they will run swiftly through their blocks, whereas, if not, a slight 'kink will jam them and a capsize probably be the result.

2d. In sailing a small boat always hold the sheet in your hand, particularly do not neglect this if it be squally; of course, it would not be possible so to do if the sheet had the whole drag of the boom, but by taking half a turn around a cleat the pressure is lessened, yet, at the same time, by letting go the end in your hand, the sheet will at once start.

3d. Never carry a small anchor at the bow unless it be properly secured, as, should the boat be under headway, she would in that event be brought up all standing, possibly have her mast twisted out of her or be capsized.

4th. In a breeze of wind never let your attention be called off a single second, but keep a bright look out for squalls to windward, and, as they approach, *luff her up* and be ready with the sheet, to start it if it puffs too strong.

5th. Never stow your sails if you can help while wet, but if you can't avoid it, avail yourself of the first dry day to loosen and dry them.

FISHING.

Boys, I must open this chapter with the frank acknowledgment that I know but little about fishing, as a science, and that I am guiltless of skill in the use of rod-and-reel. It is true that I was somewhat familiarized with the use of the *rod* at school, but that was in the educational rather than in the fishing *line*, nor did its application beget any desire for a more intimate acquaintanceship. I trust that you will not be so disrespectful as to suggest that it is usually considered a stupidity to write about what one knows nothing of, for after all my confession must be taken *cum grano salis*, for when I say I know nothing of fishing, I refer to fishing with rod-and-reel, having done my share with a hand-line and had many a good day's sport at it too ; this style of fishing, however, is looked upon by experts as an unsportsmanlike and blundering sort of an amusement, but if

TROLLING FOR BLUEFISH,

with a stiff breeze of wind blowing and a sea running is not exciting enough for the most enthusiastic sportsman he must be *exigeante* and *blasé* indeed.

Would you like try your hand at it and judge for yourself? Well, so be it.

Now then, shut your eyes and transport yourselves in imagination to Edgartown, at the extreme northern point of Martha's Vineyard, (you can do it in the flesh in five hours from New York to New Bedford, and in a couple of hours more across the Vineyard Sound.) Here we are then, aboard our little fishing craft, a schooner-rigged boat, ready for the fray. There's a stiff breeze blowing, the weather is heavy, and occasionally a fog-bank sweeps down, shutting us completely in, but in a moment clearing off again shows us a fleet of small vessels sweeping up and down the beach through an immense shoal of blue-fish, and hauling in as fast as ever they can drop their lines overboard. We round Cape Pogue light, and dash in among the fleet, meanwhile getting our lines ready. Those that we use are some twenty fathoms long, made of cotton and hawser laid (which prevents kinking); and a long bone squid, to which a stout, sharp hook is fastened, is bent on to the end of it; this renders the usual nuisance of baiting unnecessary. We now reel out a line over either quarter, and two amidships from the end of a short outrigger, or pole with a small block or pulley at its extremities, through which the lines are rove; thus in towing astern they do not fowl with each other. Once clear of the land we feel the full force of the wind and speed onward, madly dashing through a rolling sea, absolutely alive with fish, in company with fifty or sixty small craft, every soul on board of which are hauling in, as if for dear life, their scaly victims.

It needs a cool hand at the helm to so manœuvre his boat as to give its occupants the greatest possible advantage, to avoid mishap from collision, carrying away a spar, or a capsize; and not the least interesting figure in the picture is the skipper, with knee against the tiller, with hand upon the sheet, with eyes everywhere, exhorting, encouraging, advising and anathematising in a single breath—"Bout ship,"—"Look out for'ard there or you'll be overboard,"—"Let go that foresheet,"—"Keep y'r weather eye open or you'll get a ducking" (as a great green fellow comes over the bows and pours in a young Niagara, completely drenching us and half-filling the boat),—"Overboard your lines again,"— "Holy Moses how they pull,"—"There's a tenpounder, I'll bet. How's that for high!"— "You've fouled my line, you lubber you, haul in, can't you!"—"All clear, pay out." This is about the style of thing for four or five hours consecutively. Meanwhile the boat is *one* half full of fish and the other half full of water, so we conclude that we have had enough sport, and skipper sings out—"Haul in lines,"—"Unship y'r outriggers." * * * * And now, let us take a look at our prizes; the skipper says there's about eight hundred weight and that they will average five pounds. They are a sightly fish, as they flounder about, of a deep blue tint, with white under the belly, the head rounding and armed with powerful jaws; on the back in the wake of the head, a spinous fin, always erect and bristling. Each shoal of blue-fish is said to be the progeny of a single pair—a pretty respectable family to provide for, considering they number by thousands; lucky they don't wear shoes or eat bread and butter.

But we begin to feel chilly, being dripping wet and ravenously hungry. "Hallo! skipper, let's shake out the reefs and square away for home." "All right, but I've a notion to try the inlet, its ten miles round the cape and not over two through yon opening." "Jerusalem, skipper! you don't dream of shoving her through that broken water do you? Why the seas are breaking straight across! This boat will never do it." "Wall! I reckon we'll try," says the skipper, "we'll save a couple of hours by it and she'll go through it like a duck, with this breeze a-beam, there's lots of water, it's only the rip that makes it break." "Now then, haul in the head sheets a bit." "So!" "Belay that." Hold on, we may as well shake out them reefs, she'll go in all the easier." "Now then, lay low!"

As we head in for the opening the seas increase in size and crest spitefully: "See that old chap! he looks as if he were coming for us in good earnest."—"By George! if the wind *should* die out," mildly suggests a voice at the bottom of the boat! "If it does we won't go blue-fishing very soon again," says another. 'Mid such exclamations we fairly boil along, the seas lifting their ugly noses, white with foam, on every side of us, the skipper meanwhile exhorting us to keep quiet, and to see to it that the sheets are well made fast; keeping his eye steadily fixed on the channel, and in a few moments luffs up under the lee of the bar, in smooth water. * * * *

Martha's Vineyard is the Paradise and general rendezvous of fishermen, and immense quantities of sea-bass as well as blue-fish are taken there. Fishing smacks there congregate from every part of the sound, and filling up their *wells* carry the

live fish to all the little towns along the Sound,
even as far south as New York. Another great
attraction there is the

SWORD FISHING.

These sword-fish are not only immensely large,
weighing from 500 to 750 lbs., but are greatly
prized for the table ; their flesh is of a pinkish
hue, somewhat resembling the salmon in appearance and flavor.   The novelty and excitement of
the chase attracts great numbers of aspirants
each year and all the Vineyard boats are fitted
for the pursuit.   The fish are sailed upon like
the whale, the fisherman standing in the eyes of
the boat, with one foot upon an out-rigger, which
is firmly fixed and projecting some three feet
over the bow; thus, with harpoon poised, and
grasping the forestay to steady himself, he aims
for a spot just abaft the neck and lets drive, and
as soon as the iron enters the flesh (the line
which is attached to it being previously coiled in
a tub, the end being passed through its bottom
and knotted), he sounds at once, but the tub
being hove overboard of course floats, and being
towed by the line, always indicates the position
of the fish, and as he comes to the surface again
the fisherman stands ready to give him his "coup

de grace," with a lance. The chase is very exciting, but I believe the fish are becoming scarce.
No-Man's-Land and Montauk Point are considered
the best ground.

No fish affords greater sport to the enthusiastic fisherman than the striped-bass ; its pluck,
strength and endurance testing the skill and cun-
ning of the most accomplished in the gentle art;
abounding, as it does, from Maine to the Capes
of the Virginias, off the coasts as well as in the
rivers and estuaries, it may be successfully
sought almost at our very doors. We, living in
New York, may troll for it through the tortuous
passes of Hell-gate, or angle for it in Spuyten
Duyvil Creek, through the Kill-von-Kuhl, or indeed
almost anywhere in our great bay. This beautiful fish weighs from ½ to 40 lbs., and affords sport
proportionately to its weight. It would be difficult to indicate the proper time of tide to pur-
sue it, as different localities and different bottoms
require various stages of tide, the best bait being, in spring, shrimp ; later, soft shell and
shedder crab and soft shell clams. For coast fishing, when the fish run from 20 to 30 lbs., the Menhaden is exclusively used. Old fishermen tell
7

me that the best tackle for small bass consists of a light rod about 10 ft. long, moderately stiff, with a German silver reel without stop or check ; the line small, about the size usually used for brook trout, from 400 to 500 ft. long, float of solid cork, which, together with the sinker, should be suited to the depth of water and strength of tide.

It would be absurd to attempt any suggestions as to how to play your fish or capture him, for a few days' experience with a good fisherman would teach you more than would a volume of written advice. There are men in every community who are passionately fond of this sport, and who are always glad to initiate a beginner for a small daily gratuity. At Hell-gate there are men with bait and gear for trolling always on hand to take one to the best ground, and all along the Sound and indeed the coast, wherever there is fishing, there is sure to be accommodation in the way of boats and bait.

The great ambition of the angler, however, is to capture the larger sized fish which abound along the coast of the Eastern states and throughout the Sound—Newport, Narragansett, Cuttyhunk, the Isle of Shoals and the Vineyard Islands being favorite places of resort for the striped-bass fishermen, and here the fish will run from 25 to

40 lbs. in weight. Not only the desire to capture the monstrous fish, but the total change from the monotony and drudgery of business, the invigorating breeze, the mildness and beauty of the scenery, and the surf surging up upon the rocky headlands, all lend an inexplicable exhilaration to the city man, who, throwing off all care, enters with ardor into the enjoyment of the sport with as much coolness and patience, as much skill and dexterity, as in the solution of the knotiest point in law or in finances; indeed, nothing can be more soothing to the brain, that for months and months has been worked to its utmost capacity, than the entire abandon of such a life among such scenery, while the consummate finesse which conquers this monstrous beauty, with the help only of a rod scarce thicker than a riding switch, and with a line but little stouter than a silken thread, affords a sufficient stimulant to the latent ambition, which for the time being only is smothered. To the uninitiated it is a matter of astonishment to listen to the bass fisherman of those localities dilate upon the merits of his tackle and fishing appliances—the care and judgment exercised in the selection of his rod, both as to make and material (each joint being frequently of a different species of wood, the

make and shape of the hooks, their temper and peculiar bend, the material of the line, the peculiar twist, whether of braided silk or linen, the form and weight of sinkers and floats, etc., etc. But gradually astonishment yields to a desire to become more intimately acquainted with its intricacies and to partake of the delights of a sport which has become invested with the dignity of a science. If I remember rightly, the tackle used at Newport for the capture of the striped-bass consists of a bamboo rod, stout and light, fitted with a reel of superior make, running on jewels, without checks or stops, and running out 300 to 400 yards of line; the lines are usually of linen and hawser laid to prevent kinking; the silken is not used. The hook with the Kinsey-point and sproat-bend is said to be the favorite. The Menhaden, which is the bait used, is often fastened to the hook.

To those of us who can not spare more than a day at a time from our business, and who are not adepts in the gentle art,

THE WEAK-FISH

furnishes no end of diversion, both to those who fish with rod-and-reel and those who confine themselves to the hand-line.

The weak-fish appear in immense numbers, early in May, in the mouths of our rivers, in our bay and estuaries, but is essentially a salt-water fish, and although easily killed he is very gamey, taking the hook savagely.

We denizens of the great city may fish for them successfully almost anywhere in the lower bay, in the kills between Staten Island and the Jersey shore, or in Prince's Bay at the mouth of the Raritan River; but they are in no wise confined to these localities, as they abound throughout the Vineyard and Long Island Sounds, and at the mouth of the Chesapeake. These fish, arriving in the early spring, remain until the latter part of October, and weigh, late in the fall, as high as ten pounds, although the average would not exceed four pounds. It is a sightly fish, of a grayish hue, with dark spots and yellowish belly, and its flesh is white, mealy and very palatable. The usual tackle, when fishing with a rod, is a very light, short rod and reel, with a couple of hundred feet of linen line and a light swivel sinker, the hooks of course varying in size with the weight of the fish which happen to be biting at the time.

The smaller fish I have always found bite best at shrimp, which can be taken in any quantity

along the meadows, at low tide, but the larger
fish prefer the shedder and the soft-shell crab
and clams.

It would be quite impossible to designate the
best time to fish, so far as the stages of the tide
go, as it altogether depends upon the locality.
At the mouth of the Raritan for instance, slack-
water and the young flood is the best, in other
places the second half of the flood, and again in
other localities they bite best on the ebb. Early
in the season they seem in some places to frequent the deeper water of the channel, and later
to confine themselves to the flats. The fishermen of the locality will always, however, give
you the most reliable advice on this head. A
freshet or a cold easterly storm will drive them
out of the mouth of the river.

THE SHEEPSHEAD

is a thoroughly game fish and gets its name
from the similarity of its jaw to that of a sheep.
This fish comes to us in late spring and remains
till frost, and ranges, like the wheat-fish, our
bays and estuaries from New England to the
capes of the Chesapeake. Its weight will average three pounds, but it runs up in the fall of
the year to fifteen pounds, and is prized very

highly for the table, always fetching a high price in market ; its food consists of mussels and clams, which its powerful jaws crush with the greatest ease, and consequently their favorite resort is where these crustacæ abound, and it is a frequent custom with fishermen, in order to attract them, to dump large quantities of mussels in convenient places. Off Rockaway is a famous place for sheepshead, and very accessible by rail from the city, and boats and tackle are always obtainable at a moment's notice. Various places on the Sound too, almost as accessible, and Barnegat Inlet, are much frequented by those fond of the sport.

Anglers seem to prefer a very heavy, short rod, with large reel with four or five hundred feet of line, a heavy sinker, and the leaders sufficiently above it as to be entirely clear of it as it grazes the bottom ; the snells should be of wire, and the hooks used are of various patterns, but should be of the best tempered material and very sharp, as the mouth of this fish is exceedingly hard. In fishing with the hand-line, the length of which must be determined by the depth of water, although it should be as long as a strong arm can heave it astern of a boat, the sinker should be made fast to its *end*, and the leaders with wire snells, at a considerable distance from it and apart, so that they may play freely.

Shedder crabs are the most attractive bait, and when they cannot be got, the soft-shell clam will allure them.

THE SEA BASS

abounds along our entire coast, and is altogether better known than any other table fish. It is eagerly sought after both by professional and amateur fishermen, and great numbers are taken every year. These fish appear in large shoals off the coast and are to be found in the mouths of our harbors and in our estuaries. They vary in weight from one to seven pounds, according to the season, and are considered by anglers a game fish; the bait generally used being shrimp, shedder and clams, and they usually bite the best at slack water. These fish hover about sunken wrecks, and the coast fishermen have ranges along shore by which they go with great precision to these grounds and take them in large quantities. Probably no fish affords more sport to the denizens of New York City, excursion boats leaving daily for the banks, and frequently the passengers come home laden with spoil.

TROUT FISHING.

It seems not a little strange to those without the pale of the craft piscatorial, that those brawny, stalwart fishers who brave the pitiless storms of the New England coast angling for striped bass, and wade the icy currents of the Canadian rivers waist deep, in the early spring, in quest of salmon, who, with reefed sail, troll through a rolling sea for blue-fish, should find such exquisite delight in casting a fly into a quiet pool scarce knee-deep, and in bringing therefrom a little trout weighing a pound or so, or more frequently only a few ounces; yet such is the truth nevertheless, and the speckled brook-trout, although abounding in almost every brook, rivulet and mountain stream throughout the country, stands preëminent in the estimation of the disciples of Isaac Walton; its peerless beauty, its coyness, its lightning swiftness, its fastidiousness as to bait, the circumstances under which it is pursued and the locality, leading the angler now amid the most charming landscape, again through the wildest and most magnificent scenery—all lend it an inexpressible charm, not to mention the exquisite delicacy of the fish—which renders it a *bonne-bouche* to the gourmand or to the grosser appetite of the countryman.

7*

Although in the pursuit of the trout the very highest appliances of the art are brought into requisition, and the nicest and most discriminating judgment used on the part of the professional angler, still it not unfrequently happens that the bare-legged school boy, with his light hickory pole, his twine line, and bent pin-hook, will draw from their haunts the scaled beauties, when the most tempting flies thrown with the most artistic skill will fail to seduce them. Indeed, I myself remember when a boy passing a few weeks in Warren Co. in the State of New York, among the chain of small lakes in the upper part of the county, and being chaperoned by a youthful giant to the manor born, who was wont to arm me with a rod cut on the banks of the streams flowing into the lakes, and attaching thereto a common line armed with a hook bought at the village store and baited with angle-worm, fly or grasshopper, and then being bidden to follow him waist-deep in the stream, the inevitable result would be a magnificent string of trout weighing from 1 to 3 lbs.; all this we looked upon as a matter of course, never dreaming then how enviable was our success, or the enthusiasm with which it would have been greeted by the lover of the gentle art.

Although trout are taken with numerous grub and angle worms, still frequently all these will fail, and a brilliant colored imitation of a fly will lure them, and herein largely consists the science of the fishermen in judging what style of fly is appropriate to a peculiar state of the atmosphere or locality. The brightness or dullness of the day, the clearness or otherwise of the water, and the appetite of the fish, have all to be taken into consideration; indeed, the fisherman can not have too great a variety of flies—which, by the way, can be bought in any of our large cities.

The ambition of all aspiring anglers is to cast a fly well and gracefully—of course this requires long practice, and should at first be attempted with a short line, which should be gradually lengthened—and the cast should be so made that it should lie straight on the surface of the water, with no slack or bend in it, and it should fall as soft as a feather, and, as the expert whip flicks a fly from off the flank of the leader of his four-in-hand, so should the expert angler be able to lay out his thirty feet of line as deftly and as precisely on the very spot where he wishes it to drop.

THE PICKEREL, OR PIKE,

from what I can learn, is one and the same kind

of fish, although to the naturalist they may be quite distinct. I fancy, however, they are of one and the same family, and as they inhabit all the fresh water ponds and small lakes of the Northern States, they perhaps are more generally known to our boys than any fish that swim. They are essentially a game fish, and highly prized for the table as well, although, from the fact that they affect sluggish water, and delight to live among lilies and water plants, to me, at least, they have a muddy flavor, which is anything but agreeable. The light hickory pole, and an angle worm bait, in the hands of the wide-awake country lad, is very effective in seducing them from the lily beds, and this fact is often successfully varied by the substitution of a minnow or small live frog, which appears at times irresistible.

In extensive ponds and small lakes trolling is frequently resorted to, and is a delightful pastime, and many and various are the rigs adopted. The revolving squids, either of metal or of counterfeit minnows or shiners, with a gang of three small hooks, is a favorite device, and as one sculls along gently, the fish rapidly revolving on the surface of the water would seem irresistible to the wary pike.

I must now bring this desultory, and, I fear, not very instructive or satisfactory talk about fish to a close, by reviving the following article, which I wrote for and was published in the *Turf, Field and Farm*, under date of July 13, 1870, and entitled:

FISHING IN BARNEGAT BAY.

EDITORS TURF, FIELD AND FARM: Have you, Mr. TURF, or you, Mr. FIELD, any children? And if you have, do you not occasionally experience a distressing conflict between filial affection on the one hand, and your sporting proclivities on the other? However, it's neither here nor there whether you have or not. I have, and on a very recent occasion, too; and it was on the first day of July, and in this wise: I had fully determined upon visiting a certain swamp, located within the County of Middlesex, State of New Jersey, armed with my Westly-Richards, and accompanied by a setter friend, loaned for the occasion, with the intention of doing bodily harm to such woodcock as I had been confidently assured by a youthful clown of sporting tendencies, living in the vicinity, then and there existed. Are either you or Mr. FIELD given to summer cock shooting? Have you looked for-

ward to the advent of the glorious Fourth, the
natal day of our independence, Hail Columbia,
and all the rest of it, simply as indicative of the
period when said cocks might be legally slain?
Have you longed for and dreamed of said feast
day, as a day to be set apart and sacred to a
good woodcock hunt? Well, I have, if you
haven't, and I did on this particular occasion.
Said Westly-Richards was duly inspected, the
said setter was never in better condition, never
more eager for the fray. *Mais, l'homme propose
et Dieu dispose*, as Crapaud would say, for just
then, by most diabolical chance, it occurred to
my three, aged nine, twelve and fourteen, that
last year I had solemnly promised at this festive
season to take them for a "big fish" to Barnegat Bay.

Now, my dear TURF and FIELD, have you ever
at any remote period made a promise to your
boys which they failed to remember?

Have you ever spent a night at the mouth of
the Mississippi, or any of the small ports on the
Spanish Main? because if you have you can form
some idea of the remorseless persistence of the
gnat or sand-fly. Well, they are not easily diverted where human flesh and blood is concerned, but they are nothing to three boys with

a promised excursion in view, and especially if there be a doubt of its fulfillment. In this instance those three little vampires scented danger from afar; the gun-case moved from its accustomed corner, our own kennel occupied by our neighbor's setter, sundry packages by express from Cooper & Pond's, all presaged danger. In vain we discanted upon the delights of a Fourth of July in New Brunswick; in vain we offered to get up a pic-nic; in vain we expressed a willingness to buy out the whole stock of the village pyrotechnist; in vain we suggested that the fishing would be better next month—neither bribery nor corruption, nor diplomacy were of any avail. My life became a burden, my Westly-Richards went back to the gun-closet, and Sport walked back home a most disgusted and downcast setter; gun-stock fell and fishing tackle rose in the home market, and on the morning of the 1st of July, in the year of grace, we found ourselves— my three boys and I—at 6:45 A. M., on board the Plymouth Rock.

"Ain't she gay?" squeaked number three.
"Bully!" cried the other two in chorus. * * *
New York Bay has been too thoroughly done to try again, but if any one ever saw anything lovelier than the Long Island and Staten Island

shores at sunrise of a July morning they have
traveled further than I have; and if said anyone
has tasted anything better than the salmon cut-
let, filet, omlette au fine herbs, pommes de terres,
á la Maitre d'hotel, or had them better served
afloat, then he must have voyaged in the "Flying
Dutchman," or some other supernatural craft.
Didn't the boys eat. Good heavens! I don't
care if Jim Fisk *has* swallowed the entire British
and Yankee nation in railway matters, he de-
serves well of his country for the facilities he
has given roasting New Yorkers to get down to
the seaside.

Arrived at Sandy Hook, we seat ourselves in
the cars of the New Jersey Southern Railroad
and in two hours are landed in Tom's River.

* * * * * * * * *

"There's the Zouave!" shout the boys, as
the yacht with pennant flying and mainsail mast-
headed is descried at her moorings, and there's
Capt. Hat. Gulick, too. Out go the bags and
fishing rods, followed by the boys, and in a moment more they are in her little cabin shifting
their land toggery for their sea rig. Up goes the
jib, cast off, jib-sheet to windward! Now she
pays off! Aft come the sheets, and we go flying
down the river. In twenty minutes we're at the

mouth, and the wind freshening as we stretch across the bay; we shake her up, and make her snug with a single reef, not thereby, however, in the least diminishing her speed, heading due South, with the ocean on the port hand, only separated from it by a narrow strip of beach, on which the heavy surf ominously crashes, and on our starboard the Jersey mainland. Meanwhile the boys are getting out their trolling lines and squids—and here we are close upon the inlet, the great white shaft, known as Barnegat lighthouse, rearing its head from its Southern bank. But there's no time to look at lighthouses, for the eldest boy is tugging might and main, trying to haul in a ten-pound blue fish, which is throwing itself high out of water in its efforts to escape. "I have got one too!" sings out No. 3, "and, by golly, so have I!" yells No. 2. "Luff her up a bit, Hat, or she will drag them over-board!" "Look out for that hook, you young porcupine!" "Oh, Dad, only look at these two whoppers on my line!" "Hurrah! see mine, too! Such a kettle of fish!" "Mind your helm, there, or she'll jibe!" —and then the lines foul. * * * * That's about the style of thing for about a couple of hours, culminating in a score of big fellows

flopping about the cock-pit lively as crickets.
Such yawing and jawing, such tacking and
hacking, such jibes and such jibing, such shouts
of triumph as a big one would come over the
side, such yells of despair as one would fall the
wrong side of the gunwale.

"Now, then, you boys, drop those deck buc-
kets over the side and wash her down. Come!
lively's the word! Hat, you and I will take a
pipe. Here, Schuyler, ease off that sheet, and
mind you steer her steady; get the jib-stay on
that sand hammock on the port bow, and keep
it there, and you'll be all right."

"Aye, aye, Sir," sings out the embryo admiral.

That night we spend at Cox's gunning-house
—a good bath, a good supper, and—well, we
dont know about the beds, for we are off to
sleep in a jiffy, reeling it off at the rate of fifteen
knots, snorting like a shoal of porpoises.

Next day we try the still fishing. The sheepshead bite fitfully, the wheat-fish fairly, and the
bass so-so; but together they give us good sport,
and as we occasionally change our ground, we
have some fine sailing, on and off the wind, and
now and then varied by a trial of speed with
one of the bay boats. The sheepshead, feeding
upon mussels dumped into the bay to attract

them, are a game fish, and afford good sport. The bass are small and plentiful. The wheat-fish abound, average 4 to 6 lbs., bite spitefully, but soon give in.

About two o'clock we haul up for Abner Reed's new house on the beach above the inlet, have a header in the surf and then tiffin. Meanwhile the wind comes in strong from the south-ard, and as we have to make Bill Chadwick's, ten miles to the northard, to spend Sunday, we all get aboard just as the sun goes down over the Jersey hills. The heavy fog-bank seaward, and the crack of the sea on the beach, presages a stiff south-easter—just what we want. The boys, tired out, go below, and Capt. H., wrapping his coat about him, goes forward to look out for the channel, and I take the helm. The shades of evening have gathered about us, and the revolving light flashes at quick intervals across our path, and as the little craft feels the heavy night wind rushing in squalls from across the beach, she bends to it and spurts like a race-horse.

"Keep away a little, please. Now steady as you go. Steer for that light, so! Now then, I'll clear away the anchor! Now then, shake her up!"

Whir-r-r goes the cable through the hawse-pipe; the anchor's down, and we know by old Quango's deep bark that we are at our destination.

"How are you?" "Where do you hail from?" Here Zeph got the wheelbarrow and took up the dunnage. "Turn out, you boys! now then off to bed, you young monkeys!" Getting rid of the small fry, we adjourn to Billy's quarters, where, with a glass of approved tipple and a Principe segar, we listen to Billy's latest wrecking news, for be it known Billy is high cockelorum on Squam Beach among the "wrackers," and has performed more feats in the life and ship-saving line than the whole lot together. His station-house is a model, his boats are always the first in the sea, and it is confidently asserted that he can smell a "wrack" twenty miles off. His last exploits were taking the passengers on a pitchy dark night and over a boiling surf from the steamer "Circassian," within an hour from the time she struck, and in saving the lives of the mate and cook of the "Scribner," after she went to pieces, with a volunteer crew, when the attempt seemed certain death; "but we couldn't let the poor devils drown before our eyes you know." When we first knew Billy, half a score of years ago, his house was but a fishing hut, but for twenty years before that it was frequented by New York sportsmen of the old school—Gilbert Davis, the Stuarts, the Thornes, the Livingstons and a host of others, who regularly went down in Summer for snipe and in the Fall and Spring for ducks and geese. Since then, however, the fishing hut has been converted into a large and stately building, and Billy dispenses his hospitality the year round; in March come the ducks and geese, in June the fishing, in July the endless variety of snipe, marlin, doewitches, yellow legs, golden plover.

Billy's long association with such people as above mentioned—life-long, one may say —has instilled a certain element of refinement into his character, which, with a highly original turn of mind, makes him a most amusing companion. Sunday morning finds the juveniles in the surf, which does not diminish their appetite for baked blue-fish and sheepshead, after which the station-house, with its life-saving apparatus, is inspected, more gunning and wrecking yarns, a one o'clock dinner, a jolly good nap, and an hour or two on the balconies, watching the coasters working up and down the shores, and then to bed; how sleepy sea air makes one.

www.ingramcontent.com/pod-product-compliance
Lightning Source LLC
Chambersburg PA
CBHW031118020726
47495CB00007B/2257